Chaos
TO
CALM

5 Ways Busy Parents Can
Break Free from Overwhelm

BY JENNA HERMANS

THE
collective
BOOK STUDIO

Library of Congress Cataloging-in-Publication Data available.
ISBN: 978-1-68555-035-6
Ebook ISBN: 978-1-68555-036-3
Library of Congress Control Number: 2022906949

Printed using Forest Stewardship Council certified stock from
sustainably managed forests.

Manufactured in China.
Design by AJ Hansen.
Typesetting by Liliana Guia.
Illustrations by Carole Chevalier.

10 9 8 7 6 5 4 3 2 1

The Collective Book Studio®
Oakland, California
www.thecollectivebook.studio

To all the parents who are currently struggling,
have struggled, or will struggle with calm.

You are not alone.

Contents

INTRODUCTION   8

14
EFFICIENCY

How to Streamline Your Life
So You're Not Running Around
in a Constant State of Overwhelm

62
HABITS

How to Create Healthier Habits and
Trash Ones That Don't Serve You

100
COMMUNITY
How to Create Your Village,
Because It Matters So Much

122
COMMUNICATION
What to Say and How to Listen
to Get the Support You Need

186
SELF-CARE
How to Take Care of the Most Important
Person in Your Life: You

CONCLUSION   248
RFSOURCES   252
ACKNOWLEDGMENTS   254
ABOUT THE AUTHOR   256

Hi there I'm Jenna.

You're here because you're a stressed, overwhelmed parent, burning the candle at both ends. You could not be doing more for your family and work to the point of bone-deep exhaustion, yet you feel like you can never do it all or do it well enough. And as busy as you are, you don't feel fulfilled because something is missing, and that something is the prioritization of *you*.

I'VE BEEN THERE, TOO

I was right where you are now. Perpetually overwhelmed as a mom to four children, in addition to working full time. Chaos led my life and eventually led me to serious health problems and a breakdown (I'll share my breakdown moment that changed everything shortly).

I knew I had to figure out a way to get grounded, and along that journey, that's when I found calm. With calm as my guide and eventual superpower, no matter what mayhem went on around me, I could show up as my best self—as a parent, in my career, in my relationships—*and* still have time for my own desires and needs. I wrote this book for myself as much as I wrote it for anyone else. As Richard Bach said, "You teach best what you most need to learn."

HOW I GOT OUT OF CHAOS MODE

To get myself out of my chaos downward spiral, I did a ton of research, practiced all kinds of recommendations and modalities, pulled from skills I'd developed as a child, and utilized learnings gained from my formal education and degrees, from running human resource departments, as a business owner, and as a high-performance coach.

From there, I made a commitment to always strive to be my most grounded self; my purpose in life became to help other people keep their sh*t together and achieve their most audacious goals, all by finding their calm.

I'm going to teach you how to do the same.

You probably have many goals, including maybe having more patience with your kids, enjoying quality time with your partner, stressing less about work, and finding the *You* that got lost along the way.

Calm is the way you'll get there.

WHAT WILL YOU DO WITH YOUR CALM?

Every person I talk to wants more calm.

But here's the real question: Calm for what purpose? What do you want to use your calm for? What is your goal for your new-found calm?

Example goals may be:

- Having more patience with your kids when they're pissing you off.

- Being less reactive and more mellow when your partner is acting selfishly.

- Responding more compassionately to your boss or a colleague if they drop the ball or overlook your hard work.

- Improving your mental and physical health.

- Finding your personal joy, which was lost when you became a parent.

This book is a crash course that will help you get all those things, using strategies and techniques I've perfected over the years, and that my clients use with success. Additionally, many of the tools I recommend have scientific backing and research to support their benefits.

Life will always be chaotic. You can't control the electricity going out (which happened more than once while I was writing this book), kids getting sick, or colleagues quitting. What you can control is homing in on your calm so you'll be in the best space to approach any situation. In this book you'll learn the five pillars of calm, which are broken up into the chapters of this book, Efficiency, Habits, Community, Communication, and Self-Care. These are concepts and methods which will help you initiate and sustain calm, and will also help you come back to calm when things go haywire.

MY JOURNEY TO FINDING CALM

I've been called "The Queen of Calm," and as with any skill, expertise, or superpower a person has, it usually comes as a result of a complex or challenging back story, and a great deal of effort.

My relationship with calm began when my parents divorced when I was two. Growing up between two different homes with different family dynamics, I had to plan what to pack, and shift and adapt quickly to various expectations, rules, and cultures.

As I grew up I found it hard to focus and was eventually diagnosed with ADD (Attention-Deficit-Disorder). I learned to cope (before and after diagnosis) by developing systems and tools to keep me on track in school and college. Post-its and Palm Pilots were my BFFs!

These tactics served me well. I earned a bachelor's degree in psychology and a master's in organizational management, which led to a rich career in human resources. My first entrepreneurial venture of taking over and managing a school also succeeded, and I took it from near-closing to thriving within a few short months.

Just when I thought I had my sh*t together, I fell in love with a handsome South African man named Kyle, got married, and instantly became a stepmom of three young children living with us full-time. Oh, and we moved to a new city where we left behind our entire community of family and friends, where we knew no one, and where I felt completely isolated.

All that I had worked toward and built for myself to manage my life as a single person turned upside down into chaos. I had to learn how to become a parent essentially overnight, navigate complex family dynamics, enjoy my new marriage, fit my work and career trajectory around my new family, and get settled and build a community for us from scratch. It's safe to say that the whirlwind of change resulted in me losing touch with myself because I was making everyone and everything else the priority.

Adding a fourth child to the family completed us, but also brought a whole new set of challenges and adaptations. And as if that wasn't enough, we decided to pursue our dream of starting a consulting business, Be Courageous, where I took on and currently carry the role of the Chief Operating Officer with Kyle as CEO traveling often. WTF were we thinking with our timing?!

One afternoon, during one of my countless breastmilk pumping sessions during our son's first year, and right before the other three kids came crashing into the house from school bursting with energy, needing snacks, attention, and help with homework, I had a panic attack. I suddenly realized: *Holy sh*t, there's no backup. It's all up to me. I have to be everything for everyone.*

Shaking sobs took over my body. I was in way over my head and I wanted to scream at the top of my lungs, but I couldn't, because, the baby!

But then it dawned on me. I thought: *Wait a second. I have all the tools I need, from my childhood ADD coping tactics, to what I learned from running businesses, from my education and degrees to my human resources background. I can make this life I've chosen run more smoothly. I've done it before, I can do it again.* And that's what I did.

People constantly ask me, "How do you manage four kids, a traveling husband, and your career *and* stay sane?" I'm proof that it can be done and I wrote this book to share the tools and systems I set up in my home and life that helped me and my clients reach and keep calm within the chaos that comes with having a family and a busy life.

WHAT TO KNOW BEFORE GETTING STARTED:

1. **Be patient with yourself.** I'm only going to show you things I know you can totally do, and immersing yourself into anything new takes time and energy to adjust.

2. **Accept where you are and stop judging yourself.** You are a damn fine parent right at this moment. You're exactly where you need to be, and this book will meet you where you are and help you level up.

3. **You don't have to read the chapters in sequence, but all the concepts do work best in tandem.**

4. **Get a journal for writing prompts.** Every chapter will have a *Your Turn* element with questions to answer that will really ground the principles of calm into your actual, unique life.

5. **Have an open mind.** You will most likely be introduced to concepts that you haven't been exposed to before or practices you think won't work for you. Keep an open mind. New practices can be hard to wrap your head around and not everything works for everyone. But you only really know if it works if you try. So, approach the concepts with a fresh and open mind and just try.

YOU'RE GOING TO LEARN:

1. **How to be efficient.** I'll show you how to streamline your life so you finally get to make you a priority and have time for the things

that you *want* to do. I know, sounds like a shocking, impossible promise—but it's not!

2. **How to create a strong infrastructure for your life by:**
   - Building healthier habits for yourself
   - Improving your relationship and communication with your partner and kids
   - Creating a community you can thrive in and lean on for support (we all need it)

3. **How to prioritize your time and manage your energy.** So you're not running on empty all of the time.

I'm not promising a stress-free life where bluebirds clean your house while your perfect child happily naps and a unicorn serves you a mai tai. (Though, that does sound nice.) But I *will* give you the tools that will help make your life more like a Disney movie than a Quentin Tarantino one.

I needed this book just as much as you do. Even now, in times of crisis, I need to be reminded to lean on my calm strategies. This book is ready to be your most grounded friend, one you can come back to for help whenever you feel disconnected or lost from your calm.

Every day is a new opportunity to engage with calm in a new way. And I'm so excited to help you get calm and stay calm.

With courage and calm,
Jenna

For more resources and the downloads mentioned in the book:
www.jennahermans.com/resources

ency

How to Streamline Your Life
So You're Not Running Around
in a Constant State of Overwhelm

> "Efficiency is doing better,
> what is already being done."
>
> —PETER DRUCKER

WHEN I WAS A KID, I didn't know I had ADD (attention deficit disorder). All I knew was that my mind was constantly swirling with millions of thoughts, ideas, and tasks, and I had no idea which to tackle first. For example, in my childhood bedroom, every wall was painted a different color because I couldn't decide which color I wanted! My mind was in total chaos. Exactly like the mind of a busy parent.

You know that thing that happens when you go to switch the laundry, and on the way, you get a phone call from school that your kid forgot their lunch? So you divert to the kitchen to try to find the lunch box you swore you put in their backpack, then notice the stove is still on; holy sh*t, you almost burned down the house! Which makes you remember you need to pay the gas bill. So you log on to the bank website and get a notification that you're supposed to be at your other kid's orthodontist appointment in fifteen minutes. And later, much later, after the whirlwind of bedtime, when you *finally-for-the-love-of-God* sit down, you remember the laundry, and it smells like a moldy basement.

The fact you're burned out is no surprise. Spending all day reacting to 1,000 unexpected to-dos is panic inducing.

The Power of Efficiency and Why It's Important for Calm

As a teen, even before diagnosis, I developed systems of efficiency that helped me stay on track and complete not only any task, but the right tasks at the right time. I'd take extra-long, lined Post-its and write down what I needed to accomplish that week: homework, projects, chores. I satisfyingly crossed off each task and items as I completed them and added new items as the week went on. Any incomplete items at the end of the week would be transferred to next week's list.

These lists didn't just serve me in my practical life. There was a boy I liked in middle school (Kyle, close your eyes at this part!). I gave him my number and asked him to call me in the afternoon. I used my list-making skills to write a list of topics I could talk to him about in case he called and there were any awkward silences. It worked! It took the stress completely out of the idea of him calling, because I was armed with topics I knew he'd be enthralled with, like that I noticed he had a record time at the swim meet and that his butterfly stroke was getting stronger.

As I got older, my Post-it planner moved into a Palm Pilot, and has evolved into every latest technology of organization ever since (hello, Google Calendar and Tasks and more, oh my!).

Parents, especially mothers who seem wired to be multitasking maniacs, try to carry everything in their minds all the time, which isn't conducive to operating efficiently and makes it impossible to flourish and thrive.

It may seem like you need to carry all the things in your mind all at once, with a mental load the size of the planet (but who will take care of x million things if I don't?). But you don't. By developing an efficient system, you'll free yourself of that panicky feeling that you're supposed to be doing something else all the time. I'm not saying you'll never have that feeling again—I still get it too sometimes, usually when leaving for a trip or the night before a big event or party. But I take a breath and remind myself, "As long as I don't forget a human, it can be replaced." And I stick to my systems, and it all works out!

Following are some of my tried-and-true systems that have made my life more efficient and definitely less chaotic. By following these efficiency tips, your personal, professional, and home routines will be more streamlined; you won't be worried about meal planning, for example, on a rando Thursday night, because you know you have time set aside on Sundays for that.

Efficiency is the ability to achieve an end goal with little to no waste, effort, or energy. Being efficient means you can achieve results by utilizing the resources you have in the best way possible. Efficiency is a key pillar of calm because we busy moms have a lot to do and limited resources to do it all. By being able to use what we have most efficiently, we can create more space and energy to spend on the things that we want to do, and not just things we have to do.

Energy Efficiency: Energy Is Your Most Valuable Resource

There are ways to grow and, just as easily, deplete our energy. Kids are masters at zapping our energy, like laser tag—cue the tantrum—gotcha, Mom—your energy is gone! When it comes to energy, as with most concepts, knowledge is power, and it is the best first step to gaining understanding and control over how much energy you have and when to use it.

Elements of Energy

Energy is gained and expelled in two ways: physically and mentally. They are interconnected in that if you support one it directly affects the other. But when understood as two separate elements, you can be better equipped to manage your energy and notice where it gets drained and what fills it up.

There are four core physical elements that affect your energy and therefore your calm: sleep, food, exercise, and hormonal cycles.

SLEEP

As you know, when you don't get enough sleep, or your sleep is interrupted, you aren't able to show up as your most loving, nurturing, patient self. And you certainly can't maximize efficiency in a sleep-deprived stupor. Sleep is a huge energy provider for me. I look and act like a frantic

Cruella de Vil when I'm sleep deprived. Additionally, there are major bodily activities and repairs that happen during sleep, such as repair of vital organs and detoxification, among many other important functions.

In addition to just being straight-up cranky, not enough sleep affects your mental health. Lack of sleep can increase anxiety and depression (see Resources on page 252). Both of those are obvious calm killers. Prioritizing sleep helps efficiency because when you are sufficiently rested, it takes you less time to do the hard things and it makes the hard things less hard and less stressful because you are working with a full deck in that cranium and not running on fumes.

One way to get more sleep—and I hate to say it because I know you know this—is to go to bed earlier. Easier said than done, I know. I love zoning out on a show or playing sudoku before bed. After all, this is finally *your* time! But that is precious sleep time you're wasting. Of course, you should unwind the way that soothes you, but set a timer to limit the time and stick to it. You expect your kids to, right? Another way to get your mind and body in a space to prepare for sleep is to create a night-time ritual and routine to get the body prepared for slumber.

If you enjoy reading before bed, use a tangible book or e-reader. Blue light emitted from phones disrupts the natural release of melatonin that helps the body naturally fall asleep. Studies show that limiting blue light exposure before bed and during the night helps with falling and stay-ing asleep. I have a lamp in my room with a red bulb in it so that if Kyle comes to bed after me I can put on the red bulb light and turn off the main light to the room. I also have a blue light filter app on my phone if I do end up looking at my screen before bed.

FOOD

Food greatly affects your calm and ability to be efficient. We all have expe-rienced the "food coma," that feeling of not being able to do anything after a meal. Think about Thanksgiving, when you pop open your pants button.

Maybe even unzip a little bit. Sink into the couch and just sit. When even the thought of getting up to go pee sounds like a feat. This is a perfect example of food zapping all your energy.

Then there are the foods that are super energizing. Usually these are whole foods, raw foods, foods unadulterated by chemicals, preservatives, or colorants. After eating these foods, you will feel ready to take on whatever the rest of the day has in store versus wanting to curl up on the sofa and binge-watch *Friends*.

Foods That Are Energy Enemies

White bread, pasta, and rice. Grains are rich in carbs, which provide the body with good sources of energy, but processed grains like those found in white bread, white pasta, and white rice actually cause more harm than good when it comes to your energy levels. Processed grains contain fewer nutrients and typically spike blood sugar levels, both of which can drain your energy levels.

Breakfast cereals, flavored yogurts, and foods with added sugars. Many foods are loaded with added sugars, which, when consumed frequently, can take a toll on your energy levels. The combination of high sugar and low fiber content in these foods can spike blood sugar and insulin levels, resulting in a rise in energy, followed by a crash. Foods containing high amounts of added sugars can zap your energy levels rather than boost them. Sorry, Froot Loops and Activia yogurt, we are breaking up.

Alcohol. As tempting and seemingly sedating as having some Tito's or wine might be before going to sleep, consuming any amount of alcohol, especially before bed, may reduce the quality and duration of your sleep, which of course will cause you to feel more tired the next day. There aren't many things worse than having a hangover and still needing to parent human beings.

Energy drinks. Energy drinks can provide a short-term boost in energy levels. However, most of these products have a high sugar and caffeine content that can reduce the duration and quality of your sleep and cause your energy levels to crash, leaving you feeling drained. Energy drink, my ass. Might as well take a hit of cocaine (definitely don't do this). Short-term gain with long-term loss—that is the opposite of efficient!

Fried and fast foods. Fried and fast foods are not a friend of efficiency and calm. Often low in nutrients, high in fat, and low in fiber, most foods bought by shouting into a speaker while sitting in your car can slow down your digestion and counter energy-boosting nutrients. Broccoli with a side of fries does not make a balanced energy meal.

Low-calorie foods. Beware of low-calorie foods. They are not effective at boosting energy levels. They are sneaky SOBs. People tend to eat too much of these foods, resulting in digesting too many calories. On the other hand, these foods can also cause you to consume too few calories, disturbing your hormone balance and metabolism, leaving you feeling drained. 100-calorie snack packs begone and good riddance!

Foods That Are Energy Friends

Oatmeal. The complex carbs in oatmeal means it's a slow-burning, all-day energy source. I'm talking rolled or steel-cut. Quick oats don't provide the same benefits (and honestly, it doesn't take that long to cook rolled oats. Plus, overnight oats taste fantastic.) See Resources on page 252 for a link to my favorite overnight oats recipe.

Bananas. With complex carbohydrates, vitamin B6, potassium, and even some protein, bananas are like spinach to Popeye.

Yogurt. Go for full-fat yogurt, no added flavors or sweeteners. Just straight-up plain yogurt. And add the fruit, honey, and granola yourself. Energy plus natural probiotics. Yes, please!

Sesame seeds. Sesame seeds are filled to the brim with magnesium, which helps convert sugar into energy. Plus, they help stabilize blood sugar with their prevalence of healthy fat and fiber. Hello, tahini!

Water. Feeling an afternoon slump? Before reaching for yet another cup of coffee, chug a cup of water. Dehydration is a leading cause of low energy and even brain fog. Stay hydrated, mama!

Beans. Most beans like pinto, black, and kidney share a similar nutrient profile, meaning that whichever you choose, they will digest slowly, which stabilizes blood sugar. They also contain antioxidants, fiber, protein, and carbs. Beans are great sources of folic acid, iron, and magnesium, which help produce energy and deliver it to our cells. Beans, beans, the magical energy powerhouse!

Lentils. Lentils increase your energy levels by replenishing iron, folate, zinc, and manganese. These help break down nutrients and help with cellular energy production—plus YUM.

Brown rice. Brown rice is a lot less processed than white rice, which means it has a lot more vitamins, fiber, and mineral nutrients than its pale sister. Like oatmeal, it's also low on the glycemic index, meaning it can help regulate blood sugar levels and promote all-day energy.

Avocados. A family favorite in the Hermans household. With avocado's healthy fats and fiber-filled carbs, you can count on superhero sustained energy.

Salmon and sardines. Heeeeyyyy, fatty fish! No, no, I am not catcalling you. That'd be gross. In addition to boosting your energy, eating fish once or twice a week has been shown to reduce the risk of stroke, heart-related illness, depression, Alzheimer's disease, and other chronic conditions.

Eggs. Chock-full of protein, eggs provide steady and sustained energy. With leucine and B vitamins that stimulate energy production and turn other foods into energy, it's not called "the incredible, edible egg" for nothing.

Shrimp. These little sea creatures not only boost energy but are known for their mood-enhancing abilities. Shrimp cocktail, anyone?

Nuts. Rich in fiber, heart-healthy fats, and plant protein, nuts (especially cashews!) will be a dear friend to get you through that afternoon slump by increasing energy while also supporting strong bones, brain health, and immunity. Trail mix isn't only for the trail. Take that trail mix off-roading—into your purse and into your belly.

Potatoes. You may be surprised to learn that potatoes are energy powerhouses. I'm not talking hashbrowns and fries. As you learned above, fried foods zap energetic powers out of well-intentioned energy foods. Whether they are baked, mashed, in salad form, or roasted (so easy to make and gives you that "fried" experience without the excessive oil)—and don't forget potato's sepia cousin, the sweet potato!—I've never met a potato I didn't like.

Whether too much or too little, how much you eat also enables or destroys energy, thinking, and calm. I'm deeply familiar with the feeling of being "hangry," anger caused by hunger. For the sake of everyone around me, I carry snacks in my purse and in my car so that if I feel my blood sugar go down, I have a backup! Mixed nuts are my go-to.

A printable version of this list can be found at jennahermans.com/resources

EXERCISE

The rumors are true. Even when you feel sluggish and don't want to exercise, getting a good sweat session actually increases your energy. It seems counterintuitive because obviously a good workout makes you feel "tired," but research and personal experience dictate that expending energy by exercising pays off with increased energy for the rest of the day and in the long run with a regular exercise practice. Regular exercise also ensures that you don't get winded from going up a flight of stairs or carrying multiple bags of groceries from the car into the kitchen.

Exercise is incredibly efficient, as it's a one-stop shop to improve so many facets of your body, mind, and spirit. Exercise increases endorphin levels. Yay for happy hormones! It also boosts heart health, improves sleep, sharpens the mind, and promotes mental focus. Just thirty minutes of sweating can do all that; that's insurance I am willing to pay for! Talk about a multipurpose tool for calm.

HORMONAL CYCLES

Making friends with your hormonal cycles helps aid in calm by understanding its effects on energy and therefore being able to be most efficient with your time. Naturally, women have times when we have more energy and times when we don't, predictably associated with our moon cycle. Men, don't stop reading here—it would behoove you to know about the women in your life (your mom, sister, wife, daughter!).

What does this have to do with efficiency, you may be asking? There are very real ups and downs in our energy levels relating to the hormones in our body that make our magical bodies able to do miraculous things, like grow life. This is a huge reason I put my cycle into our shared calendar (more on calendars later), so my husband can see where I am in my cycle and what to expect with my energy.

Knowing what part of your cycle provides you with higher or lower energy will make you more efficient because you can take on tasks and projects when you are your most energetic and productive. You can easily answer questions like, "When should I catch up on all of those unanswered emails," or "When should I start planning my kid's upcoming birthday party?" Use your higher energy days to bang out as many of the tasks and responsibilities as you can so you can accept and lean into the more chill, low-energy parts of your flow. I talk more about this and other physical and hormonal energy flows in Self-Care (page 194).

How Mental Energy Adds to or Detracts from Your Calm

We moms carry a lot of thoughts all at once. I am not alienating the dads, but research and experience all point to moms carrying a heavier emotional and mental load than our male counterparts. Thinking about meals, trip planning, laundry, kids' school activities, playdates, medical and dental appointments, birthday gifts, meals, and commuter snacks are just a few on the ongoing list of to-dos that we have running through our minds at any given time. And this does not count the thoughts and worries of the welfare of our children and their emotional and physical well-being, such as "Does my child have psychological safety?" and "Are they being stimulated and their interests being nurtured?" and "I need to buy shoes a size up and get winter clothes a size bigger than last year." Carrying all these to-dos in our minds is an energy taker. It's no wonder that we are exhausted at the end of each day, lights out. Head on pillow, eyes closed, zzzzzz.

DECISION-MAKING FATIGUE

Decision-making fatigue results from getting asked a bazillion questions, such as "Can I have a playdate with Jason this weekend?" "Do I have to take a shower?" "Can I get this new toy?" "What are we having for dinner?" When fatigued, I tend to answer with "Ask your dad" or "Fine! Yes! Fine!" or "I don't know right now, ask me tomorrow" or "Food."

To increase efficiency, acknowledge that all these energy takers won't likely go away and do the following:

1. **Delegate the thinking to someone else if you can.** Ask your partner and responsible child, "Can you make a list of what to pack for our vacation?"

2. **Write something down when it comes to you to release it from your brain and capture its necessity.** While in the middle of a call with your mom and you remember that you need to order more vitamins, or need to make a birthday party invitation, or need to make a dinner reservation, write those things down to do later, and that way you can stay present on your phone call.

3. **Put on the calendar _when_ you will think about or make decisions about the various items in your mental load.** After you are off the call with your mom, add to your calendar when you are going to do each of those things, even if it's in ten minutes from now.

MARTYR SYNDROME

At the expense of our own health and desires, we moms will do things like stay up late because we promised our nine-year-old we would bake and bring her favorite chocolate chip cookies to her class party the next day. Yup, that was me. Instead of just buying them, I baked cookies at 10:00 p.m. because I wanted to follow through on my promise. This backfired though, because I became irritably tired, and there were plenty of other baked goods there. I didn't have to sacrifice my well-being for a class party. Save losing sleep for when your kids really need you, like when they are sick.

Lack of self-care. Self-care is the practice of taking action to protect and improve your well-being and happiness, particularly in times of stress. It's so important that I have a whole portion of this book dedicated to this subject (see page 186). But here's how it relates to efficiency: By not having habits and rituals that are for the care of you, you are susceptible to your energy being hijacked and not being able to be efficient with your time and energy.

The hard things are harder when there's no, little, or inconsistent self-care. The hard things are easier when you have a full tank to work with and aren't running on fumes.

Lack of purpose and intention. Without a goal, intention, purpose, or mission, you will aimlessly make decisions and waste your energy. What are you trying to accomplish? When you know what the big picture is and what all your actions are in service of, it's a lot easier to make decisions and move forward. It takes out the ambivalence of should I go left or right? Small or large party? What gift do I get for my kids' teachers? Do I drive my kids to school or have them take the bus? You can be a lot more proactive and productive when you know what you are aiming for. Just like businesses have mission statements that guide their decisions on what they do, how they serve their customers, and what their products and services are, when you have a mission for yourself, you'll always know you have a plan to refer to and you'll be better able to make decisions that support that mission.

One of the things that Be Courageous (the consulting company Kyle and I founded) does is help businesses with their "North Star," finding a company's direction of where they want to go with clear vision, mission, and purpose statements and how to accomplish them. A business may have an awesome product, but what is it serving? What is its reason for existing? When questions come up about customers and new products, how do they know what direction to go and how to best support their customers, business decisions, and operations? These core visionary statements help keep a business on track and streamlined toward their big goals. It's about keeping their eyes on the prize!

So now you may be thinking, WTF does this have to do with efficiency for me? I am not a business and I don't sell mattresses or whatever. I talk about purpose and intention because when you have those things, you can be more efficient as you make decisions in all areas of your life, from what kinds of cookies to bake, to which home to buy, to what jobs to apply for and accept. "Does this align with my purpose and mission?" and "Which of these most aligns with my purpose and mission?" are questions I ask myself when I make even the simplest of decisions as well as the more complex ones.

I did an exercise a few years ago that helped me discover what my "life purpose" is. My results revealed that my purpose is to "illuminate possibility." Meaning, that I feel my best self when I am helping others by showing them and guiding them through what is possible. No wonder I ended up in HR and coaching as a part of my career. I also have a mission to eliminate as much of my carbon footprint as possible. With those two elements in mind, it's so much easier to make decisions, whether it's which volunteer role to take at the kids' schools or which brand of toothbrush to buy. Hello, Earth Day coordinator and bamboo compostable toothbrush. When I started my Chaos to Calm shop, it was so easy to choose what products to sell because I had the decision-making filter of what was the most green-friendly and helped the most people. My shop showcases items from local woman entrepreneurs and all the packaging is recycled and recyclable.

Not anchoring your energy before and after energy-sucking tasks.
It is incredibly helpful to anchor your energy when striving to be more

efficient with your time and energy. If you know the PTA or company all-hands meeting is the most soul-sucking 90 minutes of your month, get prepared by doing something that fills your cup instead of emptying it directly before and/or after the meeting. That way, you will be filled with good feels going into the energy-depleting experience and/or anticipate something joyous to look forward to afterward. Maybe a happy hour or tea with a friend? Solo book date? Massage? Nooky? Before you grade a bunch of tenth-grade papers, have a nice cup of tea, a square of chocolate, and listen to some Beyoncé. A pre-meeting mini solo dance party always lifts my spirits and gets me energized.

Self-Awareness

Having self-awareness will help you understand which scenarios give you more energy than others. If you haven't noticed what your energy givers or takers are, start paying attention. Do you get energy from talking to friends or sitting in a quiet corner reading? At what times? Learn how to read your body and mind's clues to the energy needs you have in given moments and that will help you make the most efficient use of your time. For example, you may learn through noticing that after work, when you've been "on" in meetings all day, you really need that quiet half-hour commute versus calling your friends on the way home or going to happy hour to extend socializing.

Capitalizing on Natural Rhythms

Schedule tasks that require the most brain or physical power on days and times you feel most focused and energetic. Set yourself up for success and don't schedule energy-draining things during the moments you know you'll be depleted.

But Jenna, what if I'm exhausted at 6 p.m. and the PTA (or soccer team or the HOA) is having a meeting? Read the notes or watch the recording the next morning or ask someone to share their notes with you. Don't load up your day if you don't have to.

But Jenna, what if I'm most tired at 6 a.m. and that's when my baby wakes up? Play quietly, and that's all. Don't also answer emails and meal prep and plan your kid's birthday party. Don't load up your schedule when your body isn't running at full power.

But Jenna, what if I don't have any energy anytime? Aw, friend, I hear you. I have four kids under thirteen and a partner who travels out of the country regularly. In your no-energy life, you probably still have times when you have a little more energy than not. Take note of those times.

Look at the small, tiny things you can do. You own the calendar. Build that sh*t in. You can create an environment that allows you to have downtime, even if it's in the morning before everyone wakes up or at night after everyone goes to bed.

Here's how I schedule time to rebuild my energy:

- I schedule screen time or a movie afternoon for the kids. I put my oldest child in charge (when appropriate) so I can take a walk.

- I talk to my partner (or tag them in the family calendar—more on this coming up), and during the tasks they're in charge of (say, bath time), I choose not to respond to client emails or pay bills. I use the time to do something that fills my spirit, like sitting outside or calling someone special to me.

- I block off an hour for lunch while the kids are in school. If you work outside the home, don't work through your lunch if that's the time you feel a slump. If you're not a lunch-at-noon-sharp person like me, move your lunch break to 3 p.m. if your burst of energy is all the way up until then. If you can choose your lunch break, make it work for you.

The point is, even if it feels like your life runs you, you actually run your life! It may feel like you have to do all the things with today's pressures on you as a busy parent, but you actually DON'T have to sign your kids up for a few activities each. You DON'T have to volunteer every week in the classroom. You DON'T have to shoot your hand up like Brown Nose Betty to give that extra presentation. Not every time, anyway.

YOUR TURN

Answer these questions in your notebook or an online journal to learn more about your own personal energy patterns, on a daily and weekly basis.

- ☐ When do you feel most energetic? Do you have the most energy in the mornings, before the kids wake up? Or for the first couple of hours after they're at school? After lunch? In the evenings or late at night?

- ☐ Which days of the week are you usually most productive? For me, it's Mondays, Wednesdays, and Sundays.

- ☐ Which days do you feel your energy wane? Definitely Fridays for me!

- ☐ What gives you energy? Maximize those! I go for a walk or hike with a friend or by myself. All things nature fuel me up.

- ☐ What takes your energy? Minimize those! Spending time with people who complain, and deep-fried foods are two things that just zap all the energy right out of me.

Time Efficiency:
Your Most Valuable Asset

The first steps in turning chaos into calm are learning how to be a ninja with time-management skills and figuring out the ideal time for your own body's energy and rhythm to tackle all the things you have to do. I'll help you do this right now.

Think about this: We put locks on our possessions, our homes, and our cars to protect them. Why aren't we as protective about our most valuable asset, our time?

Calendar Is Key

Think of your calendar as a handy personal sidekick who knows all and answers all your time-related questions. It also functions as your accountability partner. It reminds you of when to start your commute, when to work out, and when to pick up the cupcakes for your kid's party. If you only take one tip out of this chapter, it should be to utilize a calendar. No more double booking or not knowing when you will have time to schedule a doctor's appointment or run errands, because you'll be able to reference your handy-dandy calendar at any moment in the palm of your hand. You will be a timekeeping superhero! "How does she do it? She has a calendar!" Having a calendar is one of the most efficient ways to organize your life.

Okay, so how do you begin using this superhero tool, you ask? Write everything down in an online calendar that syncs across devices. And by everything, I mean everything. If you don't have this mantra already, repeat after me: If it's not in the calendar, it doesn't exist. I'm serious.

- Block time for grocery shopping.
- Block time for calling a friend.
- Block time for shopping online for birthday gifts.
- Block time for getting the kids ready for school.
- Block time for sex. (I'm serious! More on this later.)

I use Google Calendar because it syncs across devices, easily integrates with other software and platforms, and connects with other web apps that I use. But there are plenty of calendar apps, like Cozi, Apple Calendar, and Timepage.

BUILD IN BUFFER TIME

Put a cushion in between the events as well, to plan for transition. I usually do fifteen minutes. This may sound really picky and over the top, but I promise you, scheduling yourself a few minutes before and after each event gives you time for the unexpected, like when nature calls, and gives you time to think, process, and reflect on what just happened or what you need to prepare for next.

You can use the fifteen minutes in between tasks to think about handling a situation that's been bothering you, to listen to your favorite pick-me-up song, to meditate, or to just close your eyes in silence. I promise, it will reduce your overall stress to have cushions in your day.

When you have a solid calendar, weird things will stop popping up to hijack your day. The vast majority of those I've worked with said having a calendar decreased their stress by more than half. I'll take those odds.

ANCHOR YOUR DAY

Check your calendar at night to get mentally ready for the next day and in the morning before starting the day to help anchor yourself. Knowing what I have going on, I also pick out my outfit the night before. And I adjust my alarm to accommodate whatever needs there are for the morning and day ahead.

Additionally, we have a weekly calendar on the fridge for family, so everyone can visibly see their relevant activities.

IMPROVE COMMUNICATION

Having a calendar is also helpful for answering questions like, "When did you order the couch again?" or "When was my last dental cleaning?" or "When was the last time we had sex?" Trust me, it's gratifying to be able to point out to a partner complaining about lack of sex that, in fact, said partner got some nooky three times last week! And, it's been a while since their last visit to the dentist. I delve much more into this topic in Communication (see page 122).

YOUR TURN

Set up your calendar.

- ☐ Choose an online calendar app and install it.

- ☐ Input everything into the calendar. Transfer your to-dos into your new calendar system for the first week right now. (Yep, now. Not because I'm being bossy but because the goal is by the time you finish this book you'll have all the tools you need in place.) Don't forget to keep in mind your higher energy days and times of the week and block out space for downtime and transitions!

See, doesn't it feel better already, knowing every task has a home?

Save Time Getting Dressed

Start by developing a "staple outfit," or what is now popularly known as "The Capsule Wardrobe." A capsule wardrobe is where you have just a few coordinating pieces that can be mixed and matched to make many outfits. Find shirts, skirts, or pants that you love, in the colors and prints that you know you love to wear, and buy multiples of the same color. Rinse and repeat. The benefits of a capsule wardrobe are you can get dressed quickly, every item of clothing is your favorite, you have a neat closet, you have many outfits ready to wear, and you save money too. That doesn't mean it has to be boring. You will typically find me wearing a black top and jeans, and I have fun with my accessories. My capsule colors and patterns are black, white, gray, green, denim, and animal prints (I love me a good leopard print). Please note that I am not a capsule wardrobe expert, but I am a student of this philosophy, and it has helped me tremendously.

Skeptical that the staple outfit will save you time? Just ask Hilary Clinton, former president Barack Obama, Ellen Degeneres, or Mark Zuckerberg. They tout the benefits of wearing the same outfit every day, saving them time and mental energy. No decision-making fatigue or wasted time from closet woes.

If you want to add some freshness to your wardrobe, sign up for one of the clothing delivery clubs like Stitch Fix or Wantable, and let someone else pick your clothes! Don't want to commit to the clothes but want to play with fashion and colors and patterns outside of your capsule? Try Nuuly, Armoire, or Rent the Runway. Clothing rental is fun and exciting, and it avoids the need to ask yourself, "When will I wear this again?" You can experiment without filling up your closet. Extra win: If you love an item, you can buy it!

Like I mentioned before, pick your outfit the night before; this works for kids and adults too. In fact, in our house we used to take pics of every outfit in our closets using a Polaroid and picked clothes based on the photos. It was a morning stress saver for us!

OLIVIA
the outfitter

Weekday mornings were tough for my client Olivia. Time was tight as she had three kids, all under ten years old, to get ready for the day in addition to getting herself prepped and ready for a long day at her law office. We worked together to decrease the number of tasks she had in the morning, because just reminding her kids twenty times to eat breakfast and get dressed took up enough time as it was. Some of her key time sucks in the morning were making breakfast and getting dressed. We talked about foods she could make ahead of time and in bulk for weekday breakfasts, and we landed on cycling between frittata, pancakes, and oatmeal muffins. (I'll talk more about food and meals later in this chapter.)

The bigger, more emotional challenge had to do with choosing her daily outfits. She could never figure out what to wear and felt like she didn't have anything she liked. A tale as old as time, right, ladies? The problem wasn't that she had nothing to wear, it was that she had too many choices (a great problem to have). Olivia's many clothes bulged out between hangers and dresses were interwoven with each other. She would take items out of her closet, say "Nope," and throw them down. After at least twenty minutes of this super annoying cycle, she would end up wearing the same or a variation of the outfit she wore the day before.

We tackled this issue by first talking about what she enjoyed wearing. Like what go-to colors and patterns made her feel great. We used this list to help her get rid of clothes she didn't like to wear *anymore*. We all have pieces we used to love to wear, pieces from a decade ago we hold on to because we think we may love them again. Nine times out of ten, though, you aren't going to choose that piece again. You likely have newer pieces that have entered your wardrobe since your "peekaboo shoulder" phase. Give your old blouse a hug, thank it for the good times, and let it go. (Think Marie Kondo's *The Life-Changing Magic of Tidying Up*, where she teaches you what to keep based on how much joy it brings you.)

Next, to make morning outfit choices easier, we worked on creating a capsule wardrobe color scheme. We landed on Olivia's favorite combination of three colors: yellow, navy, and gray, and a print style of simple stripes.

After we streamlined her wardrobe by purging clothes that were no longer necessary and had the colors and patterns in place, she filled in the gaps with new pieces that were versatile and worked with many other pieces. We got the wardrobe down to a handful of signature pieces that all worked well together and mixed and matched easily with each other. Her closet was much airier and her clothes had room to breathe. She could see everything easily.

Lastly, she picked out her outfits at night. Now, when she shops, she asks herself, *Does this piece fit in with my capsule wardrobe? Can I make multiple outfits using this piece and the pieces I already have?* She streamlined her shopping experience, easily picked out her outfits at night, and created time for herself the next morning. That's a triple efficiency win!

Outsourcing

There are many chores and tasks that can be offloaded to someone else who can do it better, faster, and cheaper than you. Hiring a house cleaner is one of those chores that is worth every cent. Cleaners can do as little or as much for you as you want or can afford. Hiring people to clean our house or maintain our yard every other week is some of the best money we spend. Even a once-in-a-while deep clean is enough to make our home feel fresh, and I always feel lighter and brighter. Added bonus: The time I would have spent cleaning the house can be used for something that's more important to me, like writing this book, working, or playing with my kids.

In addition to saving time, outsourcing house cleaning or yard work can actually save money. For example, let's say it would take me five hours to clean my house, and I can make $50 per hour doing client work. I just lost out on $250. The people who clean my house clean the whole thing in two hours and charge $100. Not only do they do it faster and cheaper, but they also do it better—AND I save money, $150 to be exact.

If cash is tight, try trading skills with someone in your community. When I was an undergrad student, I babysat for a family with two kiddos. Instead of paying me cash, the mom, a chef, would cook food for me. Her food saved me a ton of time so I could study more, saved me money from buying food at the student center cafeteria, and saved my waistline from the Jack in the Box and In-N-Out that were right next to my apartment.

I outsourced work recently. I was doing human resources work with a company, and they asked for support in an area that wasn't particularly in my wheelhouse. I knew someone in my network who handled that particular process often and well, and asked if she'd be open to doing that work. Thankfully she said yes, and she provided amazing support to my client. She got it done faster and better than I could have, as I would have had to learn that whole process from scratch, which would have wasted the client's time and money. While I do love learning new things, I had to evaluate my priorities. Ultimately, I helped this person make money while providing great value for my client, I got to focus on the work that fell into my expertise and increased my calm knowing my client was well taken care of.

Delegate to Kids

Kids can do lots of stuff. Even when they're little! Try outsourcing appropriate chores to each. All our kids except for our toddler, Sage, fold their own laundry, empty the dishwasher, feed the cat, set the table, and clean the dishes after dinner.

It's definitely more work up front to remind, guide, monitor, check, and provide feedback to the kids as they learn new skills. But it's so worth it in the long run! Not only do I reap the benefits of not doing all the chores for everyone and get more time to do what I want to do, but *they* also learn valuable skills and gain independence. Knowing how to care for a home will come in handy when they move out on their own. I knew someone in college who didn't know how to do laundry. After I taught him how to do it, he stopped buying new underwear every week, and he saved loads of money. Additionally, knowing how to do these fundamental chores as kids makes them better roommates in the future and more equipped to live independently and in partnership. You are welcome, future sons- and daughters-in-law!

When I first delegated emptying the dishwasher to the kids, it was quite the learning curve. I had to repeatedly remind them to not stack wet drinking glasses. (Not gonna lie, we had a few glass casualties.) Tins with lids had to be dry, otherwise mold and mildew would grow in the containers. One of the worst smells in the world is opening a lunch tin that was packed away wet. Upon opening, the stench smacks you in the face, believe me. After months of reminders, broken drinking glasses, and stink bomb smacks, they finally got it. Time-saving win!

YOUR TURN

——————————— ✏ ———————————

Outsourcing

☐ What chores or tasks can you outsource?

☐ Who will you outsource to? A neighbor, hired help, kids?

Task Efficiency: Fitting It All In, Streamlining Chores and Tasks

Task efficiency is a big ticket item for us mamas. We tend to feel like there is so much to do and not enough time to do it all. Here are my tips and tricks for fitting it all in by streamlining chores and tasks so that you can do what you have to do more efficiently and make more time for the things that you want to do. (Which may include doing nothing at all!)

Prioritize

First (see what I did there?) let's talk about prioritizing tasks. You definitely have priorities that are most important to you in life—maybe your family, career, physical and emotional health, financial stability, independence, fun and recreation, friendship, personal growth and development, sustainability, community, purpose and/or hobbies. If you haven't already thought about your life's priorities, now is the time! What are your top five priorities? Write them down. And write down why. If a task conflicts with any of these priorities, delegate it, outsource it, or erase it from your list. Maybe you got asked to drive your son's best friend to soccer practice twice a week. The added travel would make you have to leave work early during a critical time on a project you're running. Initially, you want to say yes, but look at your priorities. Is doing that task lined up with one of your core priorities, or does it conflict? One of your priorities could be nailing this project you're running, so to put that at risk to do this favor may not be the best use of time. You can kindly say, "I really wish I could, but I don't have the bandwidth right now. You could ask Stacy? I heard she's looking for soccer carpool partners."

Multitasking: When It Works and When It Doesn't

Multitasking is something we moms know how to do all too well. We are great at it . . . until our minds explode. Although we often multitask in situations when we shouldn't. Multitasking can either make or break efficiency. When done right, being able to accomplish a lot at once is obviously a big efficiency win. The only problem is, it's like a flushing toilet. You flush those tasks away, but the water always fills back up!

The way to know when to multitask is to think about the brain power needed for any of the tasks. Never multitask while needing to be thoughtful. For example, if you try to compose a work presentation while helping with your daughter's homework, you have the ingredients for a nervous breakdown pie. Those are two competing tasks that require your brain power. NEVER do that. To master multitasking, target any monotonous, brainless task, things like driving a route you've done hundreds of times, walking, unloading the dishwasher, or folding laundry, to accomplish a task or an activity that engages your mind and makes you happy. Putting on a true crime podcast while chopping up veggies: Yes! Compiling work emails while on the phone with your mom during your weekly catch-up: No!

If your commute is biking distance, ride to work, the grocery store, or the kids' school to get your workout in. I rode my bike to work while training for my first triathlon and never had to train on the bike outside of that. I hit my step goal by 9 a.m. by walking the kids to school. Recently I got an electric bike with a cargo holder on the back for Sage to sit on and that is our preferred way to commute to and from school now. Not only is it a ton of fun for him, but I get to move my body and help the earth all at the same time!

Pro Tip: Libby is an app where you can listen to audiobooks for free with your library card.

Only Touch Something Once

My grandpa Saul, who had ten siblings and not much else while growing up in Calcutta, India, always had the best advice. Poor, living in a tiny home all piled on top of each other, he had one pair of pants and one shirt. But he took great pride in his few possessions and kept them folded nicely when he was not using them. When he moved to the United States, he started out as a stock boy for Westinghouse and moved his way up to being a VP. This man knew a thing or two about how to get ahead!

One of the millions of nuggets of wisdom he passed on to me was the idea that you should only touch an item once (or as little as possible). For example:

- When you're unpacking groceries, don't stage them on the table; instead, put them right from the bag to the pantry.

- When you're folding laundry, don't put the folded laundry back in the basket, having to move it again; instead, put it straight in the drawer.

- Limit the number of times you think about a topic. If your thoughts require action, add time on your calendar to do what's needed, like research, following up on an email, problem solving on a topic, or planning for an event, and in that time, try to get to conclusion and completion as quickly as possible.

Don't Push to Tomorrow What You Can Do Today

This is another Grandpa Saul nugget of wisdom. The things we do with our time are like deposits into our interest-bearing "future self" bank account. If you do the things now, you won't have to do them later. If you get home from a trip at a decent hour on a Sunday, unpack, run the laundry, fold while watching a family movie or your favorite guilty pleasure show, and reap the benefits of a full wardrobe for the week ahead.

For tasks that must get done *and* you are so damn tired, try to get them over with! Certain chores are best to do as soon as possible to wipe them from your mental load, like emptying the dishwasher when you notice it's clean (there's nothing like the frustration of opening it when you want to fill it and find a load of clean dishes). Try not to save these more timely chores until you may have more energy, because that energy should be saved for something that is more important or requires more brain power. Throwing a bunch of undies and socks in the hamper requires no mental work. Your future self thanks you in advance!

Dealing with Big, Ongoing Chores

LAUNDRY

The never-ending task. Laundry is such a big deal in my house of six, that we've named the laundry pile "Tim." When people come over, we say, "Welcome to our home. These are our children. This is the kitchen. And this is Tim."

It's tough to remember to start laundry in the bustle of a weekday morning. So when it's time to deal with Tim (or whatever you call your own load of laundry), leave a hamper of dirty clothes right by the door, so as soon as you walk in or out it reminds you. Put your first load in the washing machine before you leave to drop the kids off at school or go to work. When you get home, move it from the washer to the dryer before doing anything else.

When the laundry's dry, fold it when it works for you. Try to make it a pleasurable experience. I fold laundry at night after the kids are in bed, and I watch a show or movie or listen to an audiobook. Try zoning out as you fold—the repetitive motion can feel meditative in the same way as knitting. Then, sit back and admire those folding skills!

This system guarantees five loads of laundry can be done in a week. And when you have a system, you will no longer stress about seeing Laundry Tim there in the corner, staring at you with his needy, codependent eyes.

FEEDING THE FAMILY

Ugh Almighty, the effort surrounding feeding a family can be monumental! It's the chore we have to do multiple times a day, every day, for the rest of existence. It'd be so badass if there were a button that would just turn off everyone's appetites for a few days. Or if a personal chef could just magically appear. Not only is it time-consuming to plan meals, gather food, put it away, cook, and clean up the more than 1,000 meals a year as parents we have to make, but it can also be costly. Plus, we're expected to be healthy and not live off Top Ramen, macaroni and cheese, and cereal.

What you put into your body affects how you feel and how your body performs. If running triathlons has taught me anything (besides that it's totally appropriate to pee in your wetsuit), it's that your body can do amazing things if you feed it well. So, the following tips and systems have been formulated with maximum health and efficiency in mind!

Bulk up. I'm sure you've heard the "buy in bulk" advice before. Maybe you even have a fifteen-year-old gold membership to Costco in your wallet that you only use for eyeglasses and birthday cakes (damn those cakes are good, though!). It's advice you hear constantly because it freakin' works. So, I'm about to make this whole "buy in bulk" idea a reality you can totally get on board with.

If you can possibly afford it or have space, buy a second refrigerator. Seriously, this is a game changer, especially for a large family, and it's going to save you an f-ton of money and food stress. My family of six goes through shredded cheese, sourdough bread, and tortillas faster than a sneeze through a screen door.

Don't just buy in bulk; prepare food in bulk. When you have all your ingredients out in a huge mess in the kitchen, prepare multiple meals from them. Double recipes. You have four kids, like me? Cook for eight kids! I'm not joking. Send them to school with leftovers for lunch and do a leftover night as one of your weekly meals. Two of our favorite things to do with leftovers to give them new life are putting them into a burrito and into a frittata. New look, new meal, no waste, time saved!

Making breakfasts ahead of time and prepared in bulk is a huge time- and energy-saver. Some of our family favorites are frittata muffins and oat-meal muffins (yes, there's a muffin theme here). Meals are portioned out for ease of reheating and counting down how much you have left before you need to make the next batch). I also make overnight oats and silver dol-lar pancakes as morning time-savers. They get used as breakfast or snacks throughout the week.

What I love about these is that I can make them all with varying ingredients but the format is the same and consistent, so it doesn't throw the kids off too much when I change up some of the ingredients, and it adds variety. I'll make frittata with spinach one week and with bell pepper the next. It's a lot easier to be thoughtful about food and the ingredients when you're not in a rush. I love a good bowl of cereal, but it tends not to be as satiating as heartier foods like oats and eggs.

Another hack, especially for warmer months, is portioning "smoothie packs." I see packaged frozen fruit and yogurt for smoothies in grocery store freezers more often now. But they can easily be made at home (and a hell of a lot cheaper, too). Either buy some frozen fruit or freeze some of your own (no more wasted too-ripe bananas!) in individual packs (I use reusable Stasher bags) and add whatever other goodies you like in your smoothie. You can put all of your smoothie ingredients, pre-portioned, in the bag in the freezer. When you are ready to make your smoothie, just dump a bag and your liquid of choice into the blender and you are ready to go!

Have go-to ingredients on hand in case things get (extra) busy. If you err on the side of having a little too much stock on the items you frequently use, you won't be as stressed if you don't make it to the store on grocery shopping day. Here are the staples I stock up on:

- Bread (freeze it)
- Shredded cheese
- Tortillas
- Beans
- Rice
- Frozen veggies
- Butter
- Snack crackers, crisps, popcorn
- Frozen fruit
- Pasta
- Eggs
- Pasta sauce

Plan meals ahead. Meal planning is an incredibly helpful tool for efficiency and minimizing unnecessary stress around mealtimes. On Sunday, the family and I talk about the meals we want to eat for the week ahead. I make sure to write down all their suggestions, but ultimately, the person who does the cooking (ahem, typically me) gets to decide what the meals for the week are.

The first thing I do is get my meal-planning template and look at the calendar. I see if we have any guests and what our family's schedule is for the week ahead. On the meal planner doc I write down notes for each day—e.g., the Armstrongs are coming over for dinner on Tuesday, and they can't eat onions and garlic. Miya has volleyball practice on Wednesday, so I will be on the road until past 6 p.m. I will need to connect with Kyle to see if he will cook that night or if we will order takeout. After all the notes are on the meal planner, I start filling in the meals, again taking into consideration the desires of the family and the cycle of meals we are currently enjoying. Taco Tuesday is a favorite in our house and an easy meal to make. So, Tuesday, done! And since we will have guests, I'll add some other goodies for that meal on the planner as well. I also look at the foods we still have in the fridge and create meals to ensure that we use what we have and then build a grocery list of foods I need to get for the rest of the meals. Then I add the items needed to my shopping list app. All that's left is to get the food and make it each day.

> **Pro Tip:** Many grocery stores now offer delivery or curbside pickup making grocery shopping even more efficient (and with fewer impulse purchases).

You can find a link to the template I use for my weekly meal planning in Resources on page 252. You can print and copy over and over. I put mine in a binder so I can reuse them or get inspiration from past weeks.

Take advantage of frozen food. Frozen food is like that friend who drops off coffee or bagels (thanks, Stephanie!) at your doorstep when you're having a hard day. We love her.

Always make sure to have frozen food. And by frozen food, I'm not talking about premade dinners. I'm talking about dinners you've made before and frozen, and staples you can easily make a meal out of. It's a good idea to have extra nonperishable food like pastas on hand as well.

Here's a scenario when this is extra handy. Just before you go out of town with your family, use up all the fresh food and leftovers in the house so nothing goes bad while you're gone. Then, if you have one or two more nights, you can use some of your frozen and pantry overflow foods. And, upon returning from your trip, you don't have to stress about getting to the grocery store immediately. These frozen and pantry extras will also save you stress if you couldn't get to the store on your normal shopping day, or if someone stops over unexpectedly or stays late and joins for the next meal.

One of the things I love about frozen fruits and vegetables is that they're picked and frozen at optimal ripeness, so they have the best nutritional value. It's an efficiency + healthy win-win!

The slow cooker and pressure cooker round out the besties in your squad. Must-must-must-must have! A standalone slow cooker "set it and forget it" will run you less than $40. Instant Pots and other brands of all-in-one cookers are more expensive, but you can get creative by going in on one with friends and setting up a timeshare, especially around the holidays!

More Food Shortcuts Include:

Baby got beans. I buy dried black beans in bulk. I don't create any waste and don't have to worry about BPA in the can lining. I make them in the Instant Pot and add them to dinners throughout the week. They're a phenomenal source of protein and fiber, even if they make you a little smelly. A family that eats beans together, stays together!

Taco Tuesday. One meal of the week figured out! Rotate your favorite proteins (turkey, salmon, beef, tofu, etc.). With leftovers, I wrap burritos for lunches the next day.

Party rice. I make a pot of rice (or this is excellent for using leftover rice), throw in a bag of frozen veggie mix, and scramble up some eggs in olive oil or butter and call it "party rice."

Soup night. Make a different soup every week, or buy one. Boom, another meal of the week figured out.

Lunch tins. Each kid should have a lunch tin. I like the aluminum kind that stacks in the cupboard; I've never had to replace one. No plastic, no waste, and dishwasher safe. You'll never run out of lunch packing materials (like plastic bags) when you use tins. Same idea goes for silicone baggies over plastic single-use bags and cloth napkins over paper napkins. Think about how often you stress about making lunch and having the supplies. That stress will vanish. And you're treating the earth more kindly as well. It's an efficiency and sustainability double whammy.

Takeout go-tos. Make a list of your favorite takeout places in town for when you're strapped for time (and heaven forbid, your frozen staples are low). I found a great spot near me that sells takeout individual potpies and quiches. Keep a note of the family's favorite dishes for the times you can order ahead and not need to ask what people want.

Chef kids. Have kids plan a meal and make it. You'd be surprised by what even a kindergartner can pull off! I know this may seem like more work than not at first, but when they get a little older, it will save you. Plus, they're more apt to eat a healthier meal when they've had a hand in making it.

Meal delivery. Did you know that many meal delivery services are better for the environment than going to large grocery stores? Some meal delivery companies have relationships directly with farmers, reduce food waste because of pre-portioning, and make only what people buy, so there's less overall waste. So if you're looking for an easy way to be more eco-conscious and save time cooking healthy meals for the fam, this is a great option.

SHOPPING TIPS

Gifts. You pretty much know all the gifts you need to get for the year, so why not purchase them in groups versus one at a time? Birthdays, holidays, teacher appreciations, a little holiday somethin' for the postal worker, thank-yous here and there, etc.

Another gifting practice I have is that when I see something that I know someone in my world would like, I buy it then and give it at the appropriate moment. I saw the most awesome socks and deck of cards for my dad the other day, bought them, stored them in my "gift drawer," and will have it ready for his birthday in a few months.

Clothing and personal necessities. You also by now know what clothing and personal necessities you like the most. Buy most, if not all, your skin care and makeup on sale and, in bulk. I write the date on each item when I open it to keep track of how long it lasts. And then when the product is finished, I write the amount of time the product lasts on a list I have posted in my medicine cabinet. In order to know how much to buy on sale days, keep a Post-it of how long each product lasts. I never run out of anything this way.

Take advantage of sales. Sales are a great way to stock up on necessities, especially if you already know how much you tend to use throughout the year. There's Black Friday, Earth Day, Small Business Saturday, and so many other special sale days throughout the year. Again, you can buy all of your goodies on sale and in bulk. Put important shopping dates on your calendar.

Lists

Speaking of lists . . . they will become your best friend and one of your main weapons against chaos on your efficiency superhero belt. Thor may have had his hammer, but you, my friend, you have the seventh infinity stone the Avengers didn't even know about: The Power of Productivity Tool Belt!

SHOPPING LIST

We'll talk about the power of lists throughout this book, but in the realm of food, my list tip is to keep a running tally in a groceries app (I like

OurGroceries because I can easily uncheck the staples I buy week in and week out). Share the app (or a Google Doc or notes app) with your partner. And your kids, if they're old enough. Of course, if you give your kids access to it, don't be surprised to see Oreos and Twizzlers pop up on the list. With a living, breathing list, you'll no longer be making last-minute lists, feeling frazzled at the store, or sending your partner those annoying "can you get some eggs" texts after they've already left the checkout line.

WISH LISTS

I don't know about you, but my kids are constantly flinging things they want and need at me. So, I created the Wish List, which lives on the fridge door. Any time they find something they want, they add it to the list. Their wishes are captured, I don't lose track, and birthday and holiday shopping just got easier.

Sometimes items on their lists go away on their own as their tastes and interests change. And sometimes the items are outrageous or super indulgent, like a trip to some exotic island or a new phone when their current one works just fine, and that is all good. I still tell the kids to add their audacious wishes to the list; this way they feel acknowledged and I don't have to directly say "no."

Self-Care

Purchase self-care appointments (hair, massage) in bulk for discounts! Often companies will have a "get a free service with purchase of gift card." Buy some gift cards for yourself (and someone on your gifting list) for services you know you use regularly and then a) you always have the appointment ready to go and b) you're saving moola!

CLAUDIA
the cook

A client of mine, Claudia, shared that preparing for dinner was one of the most dreaded moments of each day—she felt so much pressure around making dinner and hated doing it. "It's too much time and effort on a random day to look for a recipe, get the ingredients, and not know how long it's going to take to make the meal." I don't think Claudia is alone.

She recalled when her kids were babies she had a lot of fun experimenting with making her own baby food for them. But as they got older and pickier, she found that her joy of cooking and experimenting in the kitchen dwindled away. With meal planning, her stress around dinner dissolved and she could pick things she knew her kids would enjoy, and every week she experimented with one new meal, which reignited her love of being creative in the kitchen. Claudia's family reaps the rewards of getting to be her guinea pigs, and her joy of food is rubbing off on her kids, making them less picky eaters. They absolutely love seeing what she'll come up with!

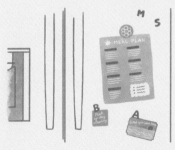

YOUR TURN

☐ Write down a mindless task and define a spirit-filling thing to do during it.

   • While I'm _____ (insert mindless task), I will feed my spirit by _____ (insert spirit-filling thing).

☐ Write down a way you can save time using Grandpa Saul's "only touch it once" advice.

   • I can save time Grandpa Saul's way by _____ (insert a way you can "only touch something once").

☐ Write down and download the grocery app you will use.

☐ What items can you use to easily whip up a meal? Write them down and buy two of each next time you're at the store.

☐ Create a Grocery Bulk Up List.

☐ Make a list of personal necessities you can stock up on.

☐ Schedule self-care appointments you can buy in bulk.

☐ Make a list of what you can and will outsource or delegate.

OWN YOUR CALM: EFFICIENCY RECAP

By being able to use what you have most efficiently, you can create more space and energy to spend on the things that you *want* to do, and not just things you *have* to do.

- ✓ Monitor your energy.
- ✓ Everything you do takes either physical or mental energy. A key strategy for calm is to monitor and manage when you have the most and least energy and plan appropriately.
- ✓ The four physical elements that take or give energy are sleep, food, exercise, and hormonal cycles.
- ✓ Put everything (everything!) into your calendar, including time cushions.
- ✓ Develop a "staple outfit" and capsule wardrobe to save time getting ready.
- ✓ Outsource tasks when someone else can do it better and faster (and may care more!).
- ✓ Don't try to multitask when one or more items needs to be thoughtful.
- ✓ Touch something only once.
- ✓ Bulk up on food, meal making, and appointments.
- ✓ Develop wish lists to make gift buying faster in the moment.

How to Create Healthier Habits
and Trash Ones That Don't Serve You

> "First, forget inspiration. Habit is more dependable. Habit will sustain you whether you're inspired or not."
>
> —OCTAVIA BUTLER

AS PARENTS, WE RARELY WAKE up feeling as gung-ho as a 5:30 a.m. cycle instructor. You'll feel more enthusiastic and eager after completing this book, but there will still be days when energy and willpower will wane. Days when you want to sleep until the last minute before having to get the kids up and skip your morning meditation, workout, or cup of coffee in peace. This still happens to me, too. After all, we are complex humans with finite energy and we're not robots!

So how do you get up and go, when your get-up-and-go, *got up and went*? This is where the power of habits comes in. **With a habit, tasks become as necessary and as instinctual and nonnegotiable as**

brushing your teeth or locking the door when you leave the house (at least, I hope those are two of your nonnegotiable habits!). You don't need willpower or inspiration to grab your keys before you leave your home; you just do it.

Being intentional about building habits that make the tasks and responsibilities in your life more streamlined will help your life run more smoothly and with less stress. For example, to save time and mental energy, I created a habit of staging laundry baskets of clothes at the top and bottom of stairs. This way, I can bring dirty laundry down when I'm heading down there for other reasons and bring clean laundry back up as well. It may sound small, but as you'll learn later in this chapter, micro-habits add up to big gains.

In this chapter, I'll help you build the infrastructure you'll need to begin and maintain healthy habits. And guess what? Your new habits will stick, because you won't be overpromising and setting yourself up for failure. In times of low energy or stress, you won't have to think, "What do I do now?" You'll just do it, because it will be ingrained, like putting on your shoes before you walk out the door or hitting up the dollar section in Target.

Okay, you're probably thinking, *where do I start with all the things I want to change?*

Good news! You already have. You are in chapter 2 of this book, and you're already on a better track by reflecting on your habits and desiring to improve them to better serve your life and your calm. You've got this! Here we go.

The Lowdown on Habits

As we deep dive into habits, it's important to know what a habit is. With clarity, it will be easier to truly understand how habits are formed and why, which will make habit creation and maintenance more successful.

A habit is a regular tendency or practice that would feel hard to give up. It's hanging your keys on the hook next to the front door. It's looking at your phone when standing in line at the coffee shop. It's saying, "You too!" when the cashier says, "Enjoy the movie!" (even though *they're* not watching).

Habits are behaviors or actions triggered by your subconscious, like brushing your teeth before going to bed and taking off your bra when getting home from work.

Habits are also things you do in particular contexts, like getting a coffee at Starbucks in the grocery store or picking up your phone when you park the car or putting a little bit of everything on your plate at a buffet. You may have noticed a juice or smoothie bar inside or next to a gym—that is no coincidence. That smoothie store owner knows that if you are at the gym, that means you care about your health and will be inclined to eat or drink something healthy. The store owner also knows you are going to be hungry when you leave. The owner is trying to instill a habit in you to have a post-workout smoothie.

We have habits in our thinking as well. For example, when you jump to conclusions, you are immediately thinking of the best or worst possible outcomes. Thinking about your financial budgets before making a purchase decision and thinking about what other errands need to be run while you are already out and about.

Basically, a habit is any activity, behavior, or thought that's repeated enough times to become automatic.

Why Habits Are Key for Calm

Homing in on healthy habits is a key component of calm, because they are the foundation of routines that, in turn, help guide our actions. Without having a solid foundation to rely on as we intentionally show up in our day-to-day, we are prisoners to what happens outside of ourselves, and we are forced to react to everything that comes our way.

Some say that life (and success) is the result of our habits. The things we do regularly contribute to the person we are and the goals we achieve. There is truth in that, and that's why learning how to build good habits (and break bad habits) is an essential life skill that has widespread benefits, including calm.

Habits ensure that what we want to do *will* happen with little to no effort. You'll no longer feel stress, shame, and guilt when you don't accomplish something you wanted because with a good habit in place, you *will* accomplish it. Good habits help you stop chasing daily tasks and instead make them routine and integrated into your life.

With the implementation of habits, you can ensure that calm-inducing practices don't get booted, and that they take little to no mental or physical energy.

Creating Healthy Habits and Trashing the Crappy Ones

When we think about starting a new habit, it usually stems from a big, ambitious, and often vague goal. "I'm going to lose 50 pounds!" or "I want to read a *ton* of books this year!" or "I'm going to keep in touch with *all* my friends and family!" These are amazing goals. But typically, most people set those goals with little or no upfront planning. Without working through the details and creating habits to support your goal, it's doomed to fail. If you want your goal of calm to stick, you'll need to address these problems and other goal-killing pitfalls, such as:

- The goals are too broad and too big.
- There's no plan with detailed strategies and tactics.
- Resources are missing that are necessary for the goal's success.
- Accountability isn't set up to protect the routines and habits needed to reach the goal.

Creating Habits

Starting a habit to get you closer to your goal of calm, and making it stick, takes planning. The more you know about creating habits, the better prepared you'll be for starting them and making sure they last.

You may be thinking, *Change is hard, Jenna! I'm scared I'll fail. I prefer my comfort zone.* Oh, don't I know it—I know the feeling all too well. But you can create a *new* comfort zone by starting small. If you incorporate one tiny new habit into your routine, one that'll take three minutes or less, you won't feel like you're making a huge, radical change. Then, your comfort zone will include this new healthier habit.

In general, people are afraid of change because they don't know what's going to happen. The unknown can be scary. They'd rather sit with the devil they know than an angel they don't. Sometimes change requires being uncomfortable. That was especially true when I trained for triathlons. When my muscles ached, I had to tell myself it was because they were doing something they hadn't done before, and that it wouldn't kill me.

You may be afraid of your family's or kids' reactions to your new habit. Say you want to take a five-minute walk every day after dinner and no one else is used to that. They might say, "Mom! Where are you going? Can I come too?" You might have to say, "Not this time, kiddo; this walk is just for me." Your skin might crawl to say those words—to leave your children out. But here's the thing. You aren't leaving them out. By taking your walk and sticking to it consistently, your kids will have a model of how to take care of themselves when they're older. You'll come back healthier and happier, and this will make your kids happier. Before long, they'll barely acknowledge you're leaving and then you'll probably feel hurt they don't seem to care. Motherhood, amiright?! Or maybe you *are* happy for your kid(s) to join you. Maybe that time spawns wonderful conversations and maybe your kids get in the habit as well. It's your call.

Here is everything you need to know about creating a new habit so you can be set up for success and feel confident that you can make it stick.

COMMIT TO ACHIEVING TINY GOALS

Your goal when starting a new habit should be so small that it feels embarrassing to even say out loud. "I'm going to meditate for one minute in the morning." "I'm going to read two pages of a book before bed." "I'm going to do three squats before taking a shower." It might sound ridiculous, but it's actually a fundamental key to building and maintaining a successful habit. Make the goal so small that you have no excuse not to do it. Committing to such a micro-habit guarantees you'll feel confident to do it and that it isn't so scary or overwhelming that you won't do it.

You and I both know that you can achieve a goal of meditating for one minute in the morning, reading two pages before bed, or doing three squats before taking a shower. If you do more than your commitment, ROCK ON! But one minute, two pages, three squats—those will all get you closer to making a habit stick. If you want to exercise more, you may think a measly three minutes of movement isn't worth the trouble. But three minutes is definitely worth it. When you are first developing a habit, it's not about the amount of time you spend, it's about the act itself of getting your body moving (or getting your body used to doing the new habit you're trying to build). If your goal is "easy," you're more likely to do it than if it is audacious. The ultimate goal is to create a sustainable habit you can maintain for lasting calm, not just a one-off that feels unattainable.

The longer you do your new micro-habit, you'll notice a couple of things will start to happen. One, your body will get used to it—getting up and moving will no longer be an effort. Two, you will naturally start to increase the time you spend doing it, or do the habit more often. In the case of exercise, three squats might turn into seven. And then ten, fifteen, thirty, and so on.

DO ONE THING AT A TIME

As busy moms, we tend to take on more than most, and sometimes it's more than we can comfortably manage. When it comes to habits, less is more. The way to succeed with implementing any new habit is to do one at a time. If you take on one thing, master it, and fully integrate it into your life before starting another, then it will guarantee success. The habit starts when you make the first move. For example, when starting to exercise, putting on workout clothes is the first habit to master. When wanting to drink more water, the first habit to master is having water more readily available. Don't try to start a habit of meditating, reading before bed, and exercising all at the same time.

CREATE A RITUAL

By creating a ritual preceding the new habit you want to create, your mind and body will be anchored and prepped for what's about to happen. Your routine, when practiced consistently, will build alignment and put your mind and body in a momentum for the habit. Also, a *post-habit* ritual that feels like a reward will help create and reinforce the habit.

For example, when I was writing this book, the only consistent time I had to focus was at night after the kids' bedtime. To get my mind and body in the spirit of writing, I built a pleasurable ritual to prepare for writing time. I'd steep a cup of peppermint tea, light a candle, and place three squares of dark chocolate next to my laptop. Doing this every time before I sat down to write helped anchor my mind and body to be ready for writing. After my time was up, or I felt at a good spot to finish for the night, I'd chug the rest of my tea, shut my laptop, and put on my pajamas. I learned quickly not to put on my pajamas *before* sitting down to write, because as soon as I did, my mind went straight to snooze city. And the post-habit ritual of melting into my pajamas was a great reward!

MAKE IT SATISFYING

Your post-habit ritual should make you feel immediately rewarded and accomplished. For example, if you're like me, you might X out each day on the calendar that you succeeded at your new habit for a sense of satisfaction. If this appeals to you, I created a beautiful habit tracker tool for you to download and print in Resources (page 252).

MAKE IT OBVIOUS

Create cues in your environment to remind you to do your habit. Set out your workout clothes where you'll see them. Place your book on your bed opened to the page you're on. Put your water bottle next to your keys so you remember to take it when you leave the house.

MAKE IT ATTRACTIVE

Whatever new habit you're trying to create, make it visually appealing. Pretty colors and patterns on workout clothes make it easier to want to wear. When I started the habit of drinking more water, I bought myself an insulated bottle that I love looking at and wanted to bring with me everywhere.

REMOVE ALL BARRIERS

When starting a new habit, remove all potential barriers and distractions that could get between you and your habit. But, you may not know what all the barriers are until after you begin. Try to imagine the before, during, and after of your habit and what you'll need in order to be successful. Do all you can to eliminate any obstacles that could get in the way of achieving your new habit.

When I decided to make a habit of meditating every day, I found a meditation app on my phone and set the notification alarm to go off at my scheduled wake-up time. The first thing I did when I woke up was click the notification and go into the app. My obstacle was this: Many mornings my husband and potentially a child would be in bed with me— not a prime meditation environment with sleepers and snorers next to me. So I kept my earbuds close by so as not to disturb them. I didn't want anything to get in the way of my effort to meditate every morning. Now I have no excuse to skip meditation in the morning. I have my tiny goal of one minute, my app, and my earbuds.

FIGURE OUT YOUR TRIGGERS AND COUPLING STRATEGY

A trigger is the unconscious activation of a habit, due to something happening in your environment. Coupling is when you pair your habit with another action or context. Triggers and coupling can both help prime your mind and body for activating a habit. You can use triggering in your favor when building a new habit by creating associations and subconscious couplings between two things that you want to follow each other.

We tend to hear about triggers a lot as it relates to trauma. For example, "I'm so triggered by my partner when he _____, and I revert right back to feeling insecure and resentful.'" We're triggered by the "ping" of our text messages and develop a habit of checking our phone after hearing that sometimes delightful, sometimes annoying-as-hell sound.

The benefit of coupling is that your mind and body associate an action with your habit, making your habit instinctual when you're faced with the initial action or context. It could be that you have a habit of getting a coffee whenever you walk into a grocery store. Or maybe you crave a Cinnabon when you go to the mall, and literally nowhere else. (Do malls even exist anymore? I am a geriatric millennial and I totally just aged myself.) You can use this in your favor to build and maintain a new habit. For example, "Every time I refill my coffee, I'll do five standing leg lifts." "Every time I think about getting a snack, I'll drink a glass of water with it." "Whenever I stop at a red light, I'll take three deep breaths.'" "Every time someone asks what I am doing this weekend, I will open my calendar app."

Triggers work by building and coupling associations to location, time, events, emotions, and other people.

Location. A location trigger is when a habit is built around a certain physical spot. For example, it's when you stop in a cafe for a salad but end up ordering a cookie because of that heavenly scent, and before you know it, every time you're grabbing your salad, or any time you pass the place, you also grab a cookie. Location triggers tend to lead to mindless habits because your actions are subconscious responses to your environment. You most likely wouldn't have had a cookie if you weren't at that cafe. You're more likely to do push-ups at a gym than in your bedroom. With some intentionality and being proactive about your environment, you can use location triggers in your favor to create healthy habits.

Have you ever noticed that when you move to a new home or start a new job that it's a lot easier to start a new habit or routine in those places? That's because new habits are actually easier to perform in new locations. In new locations you don't have preconditioned triggers that must be overcome in order to create new habits.

When I'm extra tired and not in the mood to exercise, if I can make my way to the gym, the very act of being there triggers my body and mind into working out. And by just keeping to my tiny goal of three push-ups, I'm able to maintain my habit. Of course, once I do three, I usually do more. I mean, I made the trip, might as well make it worth it.

Time. Morning habits are one of the most common examples of time triggers. We all have our series of habits that we do after waking up in the morning, like going to the bathroom, brushing our teeth, and getting dressed. There are often other time triggers throughout the day that are less obvious, like reaching for a midafternoon snack or checking social media right after lunch. Many time-triggered habits are a result of natural daily rhythms. When you understand the reason why your habits pop up at the same time every day, you can more easily either enhance a positive habit or find a new habit to replace a bad one. In fact, it's a lot easier to replace a bad habit with a good one than to quit a bad habit altogether, especially when there are triggers involved.

One of my clients wanted to start a midday mental sanity check. After working it through, we set an alarm on her phone to go off at 2 p.m. every day with the word *breathe.* Then she would place all her devices on "do not disturb" and sit silently for three minutes, while just noticing her breath. After a couple of weeks, she started checking the time to see how far away her 2 p.m. break was and noticed that she checked just minutes before it was 2 p.m. By getting into the habit of taking a mental break at a certain time, she was unconsciously triggered when the time came.

Events. The alarm in the example above is also an event-related habit trigger. You can start an event-triggered habit by associating your new habit with a regular event. To increase calm and mindfulness, for example, you could choose to take one deep breath every time your phone pings, instead of just grabbing it instantly. There are loads of events that happen throughout the day that are fantastic cues for leveraging habits, like closing your laptop and turning the car off. If you are trying to drink more water, start taking a sip of water every time you get into the car and every time you end a phone call.

Emotions. Emotions play a big role in habits and tend to be a trigger for bad habits. Feeling tired, bored, or lonely typically leads to habits of unnecessary snacking or disconnected scrolling through social media. As busy parents, our emotions tend to be harder to control and they can be challenging as we try to build new habits around them. You have to be emotionally aware in order to use emotions as a trigger for positive healthy habits. This is definitely the hardest trigger with which to build a habit. Being aware of your emotions is a powerful tool to use in owning your calm, and I am in constant practice of this.

When I find myself stressed, I use that emotional trigger to follow a box breathing technique. I breathe in for a count of four, hold my breath for a count of four, breathe out for a count of four, and hold again for a count of four, then repeat the cycle. Box breathing calms my nervous system and helps me reset to calm. Try it the next time you find yourself in a stressful moment.

Other people. Have you heard the saying by Jim Rohn that we are the average of the five people we spend the most time with? There's also the, "Show me your friends, and I'll show you your future" derivative. The intent of both is the same—who we spend time with influences the human we are. If your friends and family have healthy habits and behaviors, you are more likely to have healthy habits, too. If they drink alcohol seven days a week, most likely you will also. If they practice mindfulness and volunteer, *you're* more likely to practice mindfulness and volunteer. One study in the *New England Journal of Medicine* found that if your friend becomes obese, then your risk of obesity increases by 57 percent—even if your friend lives hundreds of miles away. Nuts, right?! Basically, the best way to make positive use of the "other people" trigger is to surround yourself with people who have the habits you want to have.

When I'm around my friend Stephanie, I eat more slowly and exercise minimalism. When I'm with my husband, Kyle, I find myself questioning more boldly and being courageous. When I'm with my friend Elizabeth, I am more creative and patient.

When choosing to use a trigger to build a habit, make sure that it's specific and immediately actionable. "I will floss my teeth right after brushing them before I go to bed." "I will drink one cup of water as soon as I sit down to eat dinner." Experiment with different triggers to see what works best for you.

Pro Tip: Try the 1 percent better approach. Small increments of change within a routine or habit you already have will also get you where you need to go. Instead of starting a totally new habit, do the thing you're already doing but in a better or elevated way. A 1 percent change is better than doing nothing. For example, if you already walk your kids to school, power walk or jog for a portion of the way there. And if that's too embarrassing for them, jog for a portion of the way back. If you already have an auto-transfer of 3 percent of your paycheck to savings, adjust it to 4 percent. If you want to go to bed earlier, lie down five minutes earlier. If you want to drink more water, put two glasses instead of one next to your bed.

MAKE THE CHOICE, EVERY DAY

Before habits become ingrained, they are an active choice you have to make, every single day. When you make the choice and follow through, you'll feel empowered! And if literally nothing else goes right in your day, that three minutes you took to devote to your new habit will be something you can be proud of.

ELLA
the exerciser

Ella and I were working on ways to bring calm back into her chaotic life. As a mom and full-time marketing VP at a large corporation, she often felt at the end of every day that she had no time left for herself.

Ella had always been a high performer and her job was demanding, but since becoming a mom she felt like she was getting lost among all of the responsibilities she had to manage. She used all her energy running around doing things for everyone but herself. She shared how she stopped sleeping well, even though her kids were sleeping through the night, and she didn't feel like she had the bandwidth to be creative at work.

She reflected on how much exercise benefited her prior to having kids and how she was able to be highly productive and accomplished when she had a regular exercise habit. We knew that if Ella could incorporate exercise back into her routine, it would help her be more creative at work, improve her sleep, have more peace and patience with her family, and feel like she was able to do something that was just for her. Four birds, one stone!

After having kids, Ella's idea of exercise was tapping her fingers on her phone while watching other people work out on TikTok. She didn't know where to start. The tsunami of information and advice online overwhelmed her. The internet told her, "Walk! Run! Kickbox! Cycle! Wake up at 4 a.m.! Yoga is the best! You must get your heart rate between 50 and 85 percent of your maximum! You must sweat for at least an hour a day!" *Ugh, I don't have an hour a day and I shouldn't need a calculator to work out, I hate math!* she thought.

To succeed, it was imperative that Ella change her mindset from one of timidness and dread to one of confidence and excitement. After all, most of the work in establishing a new habit that will stick long term is to really want it. She needed to make it fun, *and* she needed to feel her habit was doable. Here's what we put in place:

First, we built Ella's confidence by creating an exercise-friendly environment. She put a comfortable and visually pleasing yoga mat on the floor near her bed and picked workout clothes she felt great wearing. The fabric was so comfortable, and the design so cute, she enjoyed putting on her new habit outfit. And when you're working out in public, such as at a gym, if you feel like your most confident self, you will be less likely to get derailed or use it as a reason not to go. Clothes may seem superficial, but the saying "wear who you want to be" is true. You *feel* differently in a formal gown versus pajamas. Ella's flattering workout leggings and a tank top with a unicorn giving the middle finger on it made her smile. Personally, if I don't like what I'm wearing, I will literally avoid the gym. It's a thing! We all need a boost of confidence when starting something new and Ella's workout clothes gave her that.

Second, we created a routine that started small so Ella could take baby steps to ease into her new habit. For a week, I encouraged her to practice just putting on her workout clothes. And when she said, "Oh no, Jenna, it's so cold in the morning, I don't want to get out of my jammies" (who does, really?), I advised her to wear her exercise outfit to bed. They feel as comfortable as pajamas, and when she woke up she could skip the step of needing to get dressed.

Ella took my advice and slept in her workout clothes. The next morning, she still didn't feel like getting up, but there was no way she wouldn't work out, because she'd already dressed and would feel ridiculous having made that effort otherwise. She started small by doing just three squats by her bedside for a week. The following week, she added three push-ups. The week after that, she added three sit-ups. Eventually, she worked up to using kettlebells and exercised for fifteen solid minutes! But we kept her goal at three squats, because if that was all she completed that day, then that was enough (though that rarely happened) and she could feel good about accomplishing her goal.

Over time, Ella's morning exercise practice grew into an activity as instinctual as brushing her teeth in the morning. Her body learned, "We wake up and we move before we start our day." Her body and her mind stopped having to make the effort to do it, because the habit of movement became ingrained into a ritual she no longer had to consciously make happen.

Quitting Habits

There are habits we want to start doing, like maybe drinking a glass of
water in the morning, and habits we want to replace with something
else or stop entirely, like downing a bag of Skittles as an afternoon snack.
What's important to note is that when you approach a bad habit, it is
almost impossible to just quit. The best approach is to replace it with
something else. For example, if you want to stop drinking coffee in the
mornings, replace it with another hot elixir, like tea.

AVOID FEEDING THE HABIT

One way to break a bad habit is to take yourself away from the place and
time it generally happens. For example, I used to get a massive afternoon
sweet tooth. I'd have an energy drop after lunch at my office at about 2
p.m. and it felt like forever before the end of the workday. Two o'clock
became my sweets hour and I was so prepared for it that I usually had a
stash of treats in my desk drawer. Efficiency! As soon as the sweet tooth
kicked in, I reached in the drawer and immediately fed my craving with
Rice Krispie treats, chocolate-covered almonds, and chocolate bars. I'd
try to commit to only having one square of chocolate, but I always ended
up eating the whole thing. One day, feeling like sh*t and fed up with being
lethargic and lazy, I came to my senses and realized I didn't want to have
a midafternoon sweet anymore. It did nothing to serve or benefit me. In
fact, it did the opposite—it contributed to my sedentary existence. So I
decided to make a change and instead of reaching for the treat drawer, I
removed myself from my desk and went for a short walk instead.

Other measures I took: I stopped stocking my desk drawer with
treats, and instead bought fresh fruit. I know this sounds "duh," but it
actually worked. I filled the drawer with nature's candy to set myself
up for success and when I reached inside, there were apples and nut

butter in there. It was sweet and yummy and super satiating! Sweet tooth curbed!

I also stopped being near the culprit at the habituated time. I made sure to start my walk before the sweet tooth attack kicked in. At 1:50 p.m. I'd leave my desk and make sure I wasn't even near the drawer at 2 p.m. It was much easier to step away for my walk at that time, before I was tempted by the magnetic pull to the drawer. That simple ten minutes made all the difference (small increments matter!). I told a coworker what I was doing, and she helped hold me accountable. Sometimes she'd join me on the walk. And sometimes she just gently reminded me of the time. Within a month I stopped craving sweets at 2 p.m. And in a double whammy of health, I got in a ton of steps and got my blood flowing as well. When I'd return to my desk, my brain worked even better than before. So long, slump; hello, additional unexpected productivity.

NOTICE THE TRIGGERS

Reflect on the undesirable habit. Does it happen in a particular place, at a certain time of day or preceding an event? Or, does an emotional state or other people trigger the bad habit? Consciously notice and replace the habit associated with that trigger with a more positive habit that brings you closer to your goals.

WHITNEY
the water drinker

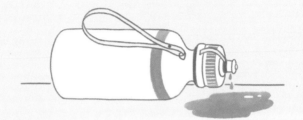

Another client of mine, who also struggled with feeling overwhelmed and constantly lethargic, knew that her low water consumption was a primary factor in her lack of energy. A body in dehydration experiences fatigue, dizziness, constipation, and loss of stamina. And that sucks for calm. Every morning she'd set an intention to drink a gallon of water, but at the end of each day she found she'd only been able to drink one or maybe two cups of water. She'd go to bed feeling like she'd failed (and she didn't want to chug a liter of water at night just to be woken by her bladder a few hours later). We worked on a few things to address what was missing in her reaching her goal.

First, I pointed out that she didn't have the foundation in place to make reaching her goal as easy as possible. We worked together to set up systems that would make it impossible for her to fail. For example, she purchased a water bottle she could take anywhere that sported an inspirational saying she loved to see, with a shape that felt great in her hand (and fit in her cup holder). You'd be surprised how enticing a well-designed water bottle can be! You're more likely to use something that you like to look at. Ella started thinking about her water bottle like a cute accessory. I don't know about you, but whenever I get a new, beautiful purse, I wear it as often as possible. And don't get me started on earrings! An ugly water bottle your kids got from a field trip with some unattractive random sponsor logo on it, with a leaky spout that spills and is too big for the cup holder in your car—those are all barriers between you and your hydration.

Second, we set up a smaller, more doable starting goal. She had initially taken on too much at once by setting a goal of drinking an entire gallon of water a day. Since she was confident in her ability to drink at least one cup of water a day on her own, we set up her goal to be three cups of water a day and then increase it every week.

Third, we set up systems to make it easier for her to reach her goal, including tricks she could add in one at a time at a comfortable pace for her:

- Keep water at her desk.

- Switch out one cup of soda or coffee for a cup of water.

- Drink water before other drinks, even just a sip.

- Put a full cup or bottle of water next to the bed at night so it would be there, staring at her, when she woke up. The body is naturally dehydrated and craving water in the morning, so that's a great time to drink.

- Set an alarm one minute after her wake-up alarm so she would be reminded to drink.

Starting on day one, Whitney immediately felt success as she accomplished her goal of just one more cup of water with very little effort. The more water-drinking safeguards and tricks she implemented, the easier it became, and gradually she worked up to a half-gallon a day, and she had more energy then she'd felt in years.

Accountability and Safeguarding (to Make 'Em Stick!)

Accountability means being responsible for your habits. You cannot out-source your habit. It is yours to own. Safeguarding means taking measures to protect your habit or prevent it from being derailed.

Create Rhythm and Routine

Creating a rhythm and routine will help you be accountable for your habits and to safeguard them from sabotage. Here's how.

INCORPORATE YOUR NEW HABIT PLANS INTO YOUR CALENDAR

Having time dedicated in your calendar for the habit is a step closer to ensuring that time is protected and it's a constant reminder every time you look at your schedule. See the Efficiency chapter (page 14) for more on this.

CREATE A CONSISTENT ROUTINE AND STICK TO IT

Just like the concept of building a ritual while creating habits, our bodies are creatures of habit and routine. The best way to start and keep a habit is to do it at the same time every day. The body gets hungry or has cravings at the same time every day, and creating a good habit works the same way. Be consistent and get it going like clockwork.

NEVER MISS A HABIT TWICE IN A ROW

This will keep you on track and you won't lose the habit before it starts. You don't want NOT doing the habit to become a habit.

LEAN ON YOUR ROUTINE

Of course, life will inevitably happen and switch things up from time to time. Health issues, travel plans, kid drama—all of these can ruin a parent's best-laid plans. Your lunchtime walk might be foiled when you have to take another pair of underwear to preschool or pick your kid up early for a "stomachache," that get-out-of-school-free card kids are constantly pulling and is impossible to disprove. You might feel sick yourself and need to go straight to bed without washing your face, flossing your teeth, reading, or doing your meditation. But when your habit becomes part of your routine, you'll have the foundation to easily adjust as needed and pick up where you left off when you're able. Your new habit, when formed into your routine, will feel like something you can't go the day without doing. And when it's ingrained in your daily life, it will be easier for you to get back on track if your routine gets jolted. Hell, you'll probably even miss it and be eager to get back to it.

CREATE A SUPPORT NETWORK

When relevant, telling your partner, kids, friends, and colleagues what you are doing can remind you of your habit and keep you accountable. When those around you know what you are doing and what you are working toward, they can help champion your success. And who knows, maybe you will inspire someone to take on a new healthy habit of their own. We will talk more about effectively communicating your intentions and needs in the Communication chapter (see page 100).

MAKE IT MEANINGFUL

Perhaps you're experiencing physical ramifications from an overly chaotic and stressful life, and that's what brought you to this book. If you create a new habit for your health or stop a habit that's been detrimental to you, such as smoking, attach the greatest meaning you can to it. You aren't just doing this for you; think about being around for your kids' meaningful moments and your potential grandkids. The moment you put the most meaning behind your new habit and align it with your deepest purpose in life, the more likely you'll stick with it.

MAKE YOUR HABIT NONNEGOTIABLE

Create enough importance around your new habit that you aren't willing to risk failure.

In my early- to mid-20s, I worked at Juicy Couture in the HR department, and I also went to grad school at night. I guess that I wasn't busy enough, because then I had this great idea of doing a triathlon. Athletics has always been important to me. Throughout high school I was a swimmer, and I played water polo as well as volleyball. In fact, I was so athletic that a boy I liked in eighth grade bullied me for being "too strong." "Your back is stronger than mine" and "You look like the Hulk," he said. After months of torment, my patience broke and I punched him in the face (not my proudest moment).

Other than that regrettable incident many years ago, I have never been an aggressive person, but I have always loved pushing the limits of my physical body to see what it's capable of. Cut to my fabulous triathlon idea. I was twenty-four years old, working full time and going to graduate school at night, and I had to figure out how to fit in triathlon training. I was already going directly from work to school, and then heading home, where I did homework and crashed. How would I make sure I fulfilled my commitment to myself?

To give my new habit meaning: I found a bigger reason than myself to do the race. I discovered a group called Team in Training, which directly supported the Leukemia and Lymphoma Society. My grandmother passed away from leukemia and my grandfather had it too, so it was a cause close to my heart. Team in Training provided a supportive environment with coaches, mentors, training plans, and a team of accountability partners to support my goal of crossing the finish line. And I could do it while simultaneously fundraising for the Leukemia and Lymphoma Society. This was perfect. I could raise funds for a cause I cared about, train for an endurance event, and have all the support I needed to reach these goals. After I told my grandfather what I was doing, there was no turning back.

I had to figure out a way to fit everything in. I lived in West Hollywood, California, and worked in Arleta. That's about fifteen miles, or thirty to forty-five minutes of driving. I decided to ride my bike to work to get training in. The first morning, I woke up early, packed my work bag with baby wipes, deodorant, and baby powder so I wouldn't smell like a bomb of body odor at work, and I lugged my bike out with all my best intentions. I was sure I'd pump my legs with ease across the expansive San Fernando Valley. I plugged in my earbuds and cranked Metallica. "Take my hand, we're off to Never-Neverland!" Oh, yah. I was strong. Powerful. Unstoppable.

Ten minutes into my ride, I was dripping sweat and regretting every decision I'd ever made in my life. "Holy f*!%, what did I sign up for?" I cursed myself. Many grunts, spits, laments, and tears later, I pulled up to work with jelly legs. I couldn't believe I'd have to repeat the ride when it was time to go home later! But see, that was the point. I left myself no out. I *had* to ride my bike home. (There was no Uber or Lyft in those days.) The ride home went much smoother and I was proud of myself, and so "I can't back out of this when I promised my grandparents" kept me going. After that first triathlon, I never wanted to do it again. Who wants to wake up early, swim in freezing cold water, and stop late-night hanging with friends for months? But then I realized something important: The pain was temporary. The accomplishment was forever. This is so important that it bears repeating: Pain is temporary. The accomplishment is forever! Since then I have completed more than a dozen triathlons, numerous half-marathons and half-Ironman triathlons, and a marathon.

Prime Your Mind

Giving an inspirational speech to yourself and getting your head right before you take on something new are examples of priming your mind to make it a lot easier to go into uncomfortable situations. You'll know what to anticipate, and you'll know that you are not only capable of surviving the situation, but you'll even benefit from it. Priming your mind gets you in the headspace of being ready for what is to come so you can be most successful in that moment.

You can use priming for all kinds of situations, such as taking your five-year-old to their first day at a new school and not knowing any of the other parents. Going on a double date with a new couple. Going on a first date. Starting a new job. Typically, when starting something new, like having a conversation with a stranger, the first few minutes can be uncomfortable or even excruciating. But once you know that you are capable of getting past those five minutes, you can truly be in the experience. In a conversation with someone new, for example, those first five minutes can be pretty awkward until you find a topic that you both enjoy talking about.

With exercising, the first five minutes are typically the worst, but after that, you feel less anxious and it tends to be easier to keep going. The question to ask yourself when you don't want to do your desired habit is, "Am I willing to be uncomfortable for five minutes?" Know that after that, you will get over your discomfort and reap the benefits of time and energy well spent.

I found myself asking this question a lot when it was "writing time" for this book. As I previously mentioned, because of work, family, and all of my other responsibilities, I mostly wrote at night. It wasn't necessarily the time I wanted to be writing, because I tend to focus best in the morning and late afternoon. But, I am a busy mom and needed to fit it in where I could. So when I was tired and just wanted to put on my jammies and get cozy in my bed, I reminded myself that the first few minutes were going to be the most uncomfortable until I got into the groove of writing, and that I was capable and willing to experience this discomfort so that I could build and maintain my habit of writing at night in order to achieve my goal of finishing this book.

Bringing It All Together

There are habits that aid in your calm (such as reading every day, staying hydrated, moving your body, journaling, getting sufficient sleep), and habits that take away your calm (such as hitting the snooze button until five minutes after your wake-up time, drinking excessive caffeine, skipping lunch).

Your life is made up of thousands of small habits. To increase calm, you must create habits that serve you and remove the ones that don't (I will help you do this in the next section). It does not need to be done overnight. As shown by Ella the Exerciser and Whitney the Water Drinker, if you 1) make it fun, 2) set a small goal, and 3) safeguard your new habit by putting systems into place that make it hard *not* to do it, you'll see progress starting at day one. One small success will lead to the next and before you know it, you'll be nailing your new habit without even thinking about it.

As you've read through this chapter so far, I hope you have been reflecting on your own habits and thinking about where to begin to create more calming habits in your life. If you're feeling overwhelmed by this, take a deep breath—I've got you! Next, I'll take you through a step-by-step guide on how to assess your habits, figure out which one(s) to stop or start, and plan your system to make sure it sticks and becomes part of your routine. Let's do it!

YOUR TURN

Now that you've learned what a habit is and isn't, how to create and break habits, and how to make them stick, it's time to put this knowledge into action! You will use all of this to assess your current habits and how they affect your calm.

TAKE YOUR HABIT INVENTORY

This is not meant to be a "Create a list of all the sh*tty things I do and change them" task. Nope. You are a badass parent and you care or you wouldn't be here. Healthier habits are not about changing who you are—you are perfectly imperfect the way you are. We all are. But the aim is to make your life less stressful, let you breathe a little more, and allow you to enjoy each day more because you no longer need to spend so much time wondering how to fit in every task and responsibility.

Don't place judgment on your habits. You're naturally going to think of your "bad" habits. But I want you to think about all your habits—all the actions and behaviors you do without effort. You may not feel like you are able to think of all your habits right now, and it would be inhuman if you could think of every single habit you have at this exact moment. Just write down what comes to mind. And then, as you go about your day, take notice. What do you do instinctually? As those things happen, write them down in your notebook or on your phone, so you can reflect on them later.

Here are a just a few common habits to get you started: drinking coffee, refilling coffee, waking up early, smoking cigarettes, biting nails, checking social media, washing hands after the restroom, snacking at night, bringing a reusable mug, skipping breakfast, brushing teeth twice a day, drinking water, stretching, reading the news, reading a book, texting your partner, checking email, meditating, journaling, cracking your joints, saving money, going to bed late, overeating, saying "I love you."

EVALUATE YOUR CURRENT HABITS

Now that you have a list of your habits, reflect on each one and ask yourself:

- [ ] Does this habit benefit me?
- [ ] Does this habit enhance my calm?
- [ ] Does this habit make me more able to show up for myself and those around me?
- [ ] Does this habit make me feel good about myself?
- [ ] Does it bring me joy? (I'm talking about real joy, not fleeting joy like playing Candy Crush on your phone or checking likes on Instagram. I'm talking about feeling connected with loved ones; feeling like you are nurturing your mind, body, and spirit; feeling like you made a deposit in the goodwill bank or did something good yourself.)

ASK YOURSELF, WHAT IS THE TRIGGER FOR EACH HABIT?

The most common triggers are location, time, events, emotions, and other people. I filled out two example habits to help with your reflection.

Habit	Calm or Stress	Trigger
Hit snooze	Stress	*Event:* Alarm, *Emotion:* Tired
Drink water	Calm	*Location:* Bedroom, *Event:* Mealtime

The practice of reflecting here will help you beyond just this moment. As you notice habits in your day-to-day life, you'll be more likely to assess and reflect on them in those moments and be more cognizant of your triggers and how your habits affect you.

How to Mindfully Choose, Develop, and Nurture a Habit

CHOOSE A HABIT TO START OR STOP

To figure out which habit you'd like to implement the most right now, start with a brain dump. Go ahead and make these big! If you are having trouble thinking of habits to start, here's some food for thought:

Exercise every day · Plan for the week ahead · Drink eight cups of water per day · Get eight hours of sleep per night · Meditate for five minutes per day · Write in a gratitude journal every day · Use social media for no more than ten minutes per day · Do positive affirmations each morning · Stick to a budget · Share words of appreciation for people in your life · Look for silver linings · Eat less meat

1. Make a list of the habits you would like to have.

2. Look at your list and circle the habit(s) that will help you create more calm in your day-to-day life.

3. Of your circled habits, pick one that you know you can easily create a trigger for, like creating a phone alarm, or a trigger you can create based on a location, like in the kitchen or at your desk.

4. Next, write down the ONE big, broad habit you would like to create. What is the smallest version of that habit that you are capable of completing every day?

5. Finally, write down the smallest and most doable goal to help you start forming your habit.

Examples:

Work out more: Set an afternoon alarm to remind me to walk for five minutes or do three sit-ups or plank for ten seconds.

Start meditating: After I drop off the kids at school, do one three-minute meditation a day.

Drink more water: Take two sips of water before leaving bed every morning and before dinner.

Read more: Read two pages in bed before turning off the light, read two pages in the morning before getting out of bed, or read two pages when you get to your desk.

DEVELOP YOUR HABIT BY CREATING
THE RIGHT CONDITIONS

Woo-hoo! You've identified what habit to create (or stop!) and you've set a doable goal. You're on your way.

1. **Make it nonnegotiable.** Don't make it a choice—make it impossible to do anything but the thing you've set out to do. The more "outs" you give yourself, the more you're setting yourself up for failure. Write down how you are going to create the conditions that will make your habit easy to do.

2. **Think about the routine that your new habit will be a part of.** What ritual will you do immediately before the habit? What are the triggers that you will associate with the habit? (Location, time, events, emotions, and other people.) Answer the following questions:

   - What will you do before the habit to ensure that you are set up for success? What is the routine that your habit will be a part of?
   - What trigger will you associate with your habit? What will you do after the habit to feel closure and a sense of reward?
   - Think about the potential barriers that could get in the way of making your habit successful.

3. **Is your habit attractive, easy, obvious, and satisfying?** If you answered "no" to any part of this question, ask why and remove any barrier that gets in the way of making it attractive, easy, obvious, and satisfying.

4. **Who are the people in your life who should know about this habit?** Who are the people who can help hold you accountable?

NURTURE YOUR HABIT TO ENSURE CONTINUED SUCCESS

Reflect and write about the reasons why you want this habit. What situations will it fix if you develop this new habit? How does having this habit benefit your life and help you create calm?

Now, think about what the worst-case scenario would be if you tried this new habit on for size. Chances are it's not a life-or-death consequence and it's 100 percent worth trying. If the worst-case scenario happens, ask yourself if you would be able to deal with that.

One tiny habit can alter other areas of your life positively. Make a list of all the ways that creating your new habit will benefit other areas of your life.

OWN YOUR CALM: HABITS RECAP

Habits are the foundation of healthy or unhealthy routines that either make or break your ability to stay calm. Starting small with habits ensures your success.

✓ To quit bad habits, it's easier to replace a bad habit with a good one, versus trying to eliminate it altogether. Watch for or remove the triggers of your habit.

✓ To get a new habit to stick, set up accountability and safeguarding. Try to couple a habit with another activity you're already doing.

✓ Make your new habit(s) nonnegotiable. Put incredible meaning into why you're doing it. Realize you are capable of moving through any temporary discomfort. You've got this!

unity

How to Create Your Village,
Because It Matters So Much

> "Alone we can do so little,
> together we can do so much."
>
> —HELEN KELLER

IT'S SIX IN THE EVENING. Your partner just texted they're on their way home, an hour late. How will dinner get made now? WTF! Your five-year-old son just shoved your three-year-old over to take a paper towel tube she'd been using out of her hand. "Mine!" he yells. "Mooommmmmyyyy!!!!" she wails, plopping down to the ground. It's then you notice, yep, her pull-up (you thought diaper days were over) is leaking. Ew.

One thing at a time, you say to yourself, trying to keep your cool. You motion to your son, "Don't shove your sister! Hand over the paper towel tube." (Why are they fighting over a useless paper towel tube?) What ensues is a nearly Braveheart-intense battle.

He won't give up the tube; instead, he whacks you with it. "That's it, go to your room for a time-out." But he's been possessed by the devil itself and refuses to listen. He starts to scream and cry that he hates you.

You text your best friend, another mama who gets you, whom you trust with your deepest stuff. Your fingers fly in desperation. "Help me, I'm hiding from my deranged children!!"

There's no need to worry about the kids' safety; you know exactly where they are, banging on the outside of the door for you. Well, at least they're on the same side now, you think, through hot tears pouring down your cheeks. *What has life become? Why am I such a bad mom who has no control of her children?* You beat yourself up.

A text, like a hand reaching through the water to help save you from drowning, buzzes your phone. It says this: "This will pass, mama. You're an amazing mom. An iced churro latte is on your doorstep." It is from your best friend. Your fairy godmother. And just like that, you can go on. You uncurl yourself from the fetal position on the floor and stand.

You sigh. You breathe. You claim your prize, your hug in the form of liquid, on the front step. You sip.

You're grateful. This, mamas, is the power of having a community.

In this chapter, you'll learn more about why community is so important for calm, how to choose and build a community that supports you, and how to respectfully and with love distance or remove members from your community who do not serve you and your life.

The Importance of Community for Calm

It's imperative to find a few quality humans you can talk to. The moment you share what's in your heart with someone you trust and who cares about you, your problem feels less heavy. I'm so lucky to have Kyle, who is my everything. I'm also fortunate to have met and worked to foster deep, incredible friendships that I'm able to go to when I need to work through issues and challenges. Or, frankly, just to let my hair down and have a great time.

Humans are communal creatures. We thrive being a part of society and helping each other out. It takes all kinds of minds, strengths, interests, thinking, and bodies for our global society to thrive, even in our micro-communities.

Parenthood can be one of the most isolating experiences of human existence if you don't have an active community around you. You can feel very much alone when you're at home with a crying baby. Or frustrated out of your mind when you're running errands with tantruming toddlers who don't listen. When your kids have a hard time in school, whether with homework, teachers, or socially in their friendship circles, you need a judgment-free space to be able to share openly. In fact, not having a community can lead to depression and other detrimental mental and physical ailments.

Postpartum depression and anxiety afflict 10 to 20 percent of new mothers (see Resources on page 252). And it doesn't end there. We love our children so much that when they go through challenging moments, no matter what their age, it's difficult not to internalize their stressors, issues, and conflicts. For moms, in particular, it feels like we have an invisible umbilical cord attached to our offspring, and we feel everything they feel. In parenting, we relive our own childhood in many ways—some good, and some not so good. Many situations parents encounter can trigger unhealthy patterns or traumas from our own past.

And then there's the stress of co-parenting. Even in the healthiest, most loving relationships, you're still parenting with a full human being who is different from you, who may want to parent differently, based on their own childhood experiences. Whether you're parenting with a partner who lives in the same house or somewhere else, coming to an agreement on discipline, rewards, schedule, and activities can be challenging. Having a close community of people to bounce ideas off of, vent to, get advice from, and even help pick up the parenting slack on busy days is a must.

Types of Relationships

As you know, there are many types of relationships that comprise a community. There is your most intimate community, the ones you share a home with. And then there are those who don't live with you. This chapter is focused on calm as it relates to the people you do not share a home with, your chosen family (outside of your partner), and the people you interact with in the world.

You may assume that your family (parents, siblings) are your community, but that isn't always the case. For some people, immediate and extended family is their community, including parents, siblings, in-laws, aunts, uncles, cousins, nieces, and nephews. If you're one of the lucky ones with a great support system in your extended family, that might be enough for you to feel like you have all the support you need. If so, congratulations, you won the family jackpot! This, however, isn't the experience of the majority of parents. So when you don't have a built-in familial community, you have to create it. Friends, neighbors, colleagues, group members, and acquaintances—they are what comprise our external community.

Friendships

Friendships come in all different forms, ranging from transactional friends to deep meaningful friendships, and they all serve a purpose in supporting your life.

Helper friends are people who serve a particular benefit in your life—you help each other out in a transactional way. You're there for each other when you need it, but you don't necessarily hang out or do friend-like things together.

Think of the mom you call to have a playdate for one of your kids while you take the other to a birthday party. Or the friend you call if you're running late to school pick-up who lives nearby so it's no sweat for them to pick up your kid too and have them hang out at their house until you can get there.

Helper friends can call on you too. It's the nature of your relationship, a mutual give and take. You don't have to go deep on the meaning of life and have regular updates.

I don't call these friends "acquaintances," because they're more than that. But they aren't who you call for comfort when you're in emotional distress. You probably wouldn't choose to hang out with this person in your free time, but if you happened upon each other, you wouldn't turn around and run in the opposite direction, either. You make small talk about summer camps or carpool and know what each other's kids are up to. Above all, you have an understanding that you can help each other out. Unlike acquaintances, with helper friendships, there has to be a trust—you are entrusting them with your kids, after all.

Contextual friendships are people you connect with in a certain place and time, but not typically outside of that context. For example, maybe you met through a mutual friend and now you enjoy seeing each other when your mutual friend has a party. Or perhaps your kid is friends with their kid and now you hang out and chat when your kids have playdates. Another example might be while at a seminar for work you met this person and became close over the course of the seminar and look for each other in future workshops—your workshop buddy. Or your kids are on a sports team together and you see each other and talk at all the practices and games. These kinds of friendships include neighbors you chat with at the mailbox, your meetup group, or AA meeting folks. Your main contact with these friends is exclusively within the context in which you met.

Long-term friendships (friends from childhood, school, or just from many years ago) can be any of the above. These types of friends understand ebbs and flows of connection and don't take them personally. Throughout life, you come back together and pick up right where you left off. Part of being a lifelong friend is recognizing that the relationship has value regardless of how often you connect.

A *deep friendship* is not how long you've known a person, but how close in your friend circle they are to you. A deep friendship is one where both people feel seen, heard, and accepted just as they are, and you feel safe talking to them about what's really going on in life at the best and darkest levels. These friends cherish and adore the things that make you unique, including all your weird quirks.

Anyone can move from one category to the other. What once was a deep, meaningful relationship might turn into a helper one, and vice versa. You may also find that your friendships ebb and flow. Certain friends go through times when they aren't as communicative for various reasons. Sometimes it's hard keeping up with friendships in different phases of life or time zones, especially if you've had a baby and your best friends aren't parents yet. It's not their fault; they just don't know yet! Sometimes you lose common interests with friends, even though you were both obsessed with the Spice Girls and Sanrio (Keroppi erasers ftw) as kids.

No matter what, I highly recommend having at least one friend you can call on when you need to offload your kid when they're driving you nuts. Like when your kid has used up all their screen time and needs to get out of the house and you need to catch up on a bunch of work or crash in bed for an hour or two.

Community Members

Like the concept of making a house a home, a community is what provides the feeling we are part of something bigger than ourselves. Strong communities provide quick hits of social connection that foster our sense of belonging. Participating in a community bonded by attitudes, values, location, and goals is an essential ingredient to enjoying a fulfilling life. Especially in challenging times, being a part of a community and having relationships with those around you provides vital social connection and engagement. Belonging to a community also boosts physical and mental health (including staving off depression and anxiety from isolation and loneliness). Having a strong community means you're never truly alone.

In addition to a sense of belonging, resilient, close communities come together and adapt. This happened to me firsthand during the COVID-19 pandemic. Where we live, 95 percent of the businesses are mom and pop places, owned and run locally. The owners live within the community they support and they are our neighbors, friends, and kids' friends' parents. Our community rallied together and the majority of our local businesses were able to keep their doors open due to that support. People bought gift cards to use later. We fundraised to keep payrolls going. These small businesses have been able to withstand the ebbs and flows of the pandemic because everyone showed up for each other. I will check my privilege here as I know not all communities were able to weather the pandemic and, sadly, way too many small businesses did not survive.

Community isn't only found in your neighborhood. Online communities are great ways to connect with people of similar interests and experiences as well. I definitely found solace in an online community after discovering that I wasn't able to breastfeed our youngest child, Sage. In order to provide Sage with breast milk, I had to pump—constantly. For any mamas who haven't had the displeasure, pumping can be incredibly isolating and lonely. I spent an exorbitant amount of time and energy pumping, scheduling pumping, cleaning pumping parts, and storing milk. I didn't know anyone else who had experienced this before or was going through it simultaneously with me.

I found a group on Facebook for "exclusively pumping mamas" and being in this group made me feel less alone. We openly shared our distresses, mishaps, frustrations, triumphs, and everything in between with each other—knowing that we all shared the same experience of not being able to feed our child directly with our bodies and feeling the guilt that often comes with it. We had each other for support as we struggled through what we were missing (for whatever the reason was).

One time a sneaky little fly flew straight into a fresh batch of warm liquid gold (breast milk). Could I still use it? I immediately took a picture, took out the fly, and posted the image to the group, asking if anyone else had experienced this and their thoughts on whether it was okay to feed this milk to my baby. There were mixed responses, but ultimately I didn't feel so alone going through such an intimate and challenging moment. (By the way, I did not end up feeding the fly milk to Sage. He was still a newborn, I had plenty of other milk for him, and I didn't want to take a chance of him getting sick.)

A client of mine, Brianne the Betrayed, found solace in an online group as well. Her wife had an affair, and she didn't want to tell people close to her because she wasn't sure what she wanted to do with the future of their marriage. So she found a Facebook group that was filled with other women who had been through the same thing. Some stayed with their partners and others didn't. Brianne knew that if she told her family and friends about the event, they would all have their own opinions about what she should do and would most likely try to pressure her into doing what they thought was right, rather than what she wanted to do. The online community she found provided objective support, open-mindedness, and a place for her to share her story openly without personal judgment or subjective pressure. She was able to make her decision about the future of her relationship—which was to let it go—from a place of calm and conviction instead of from external pressures.

How to Be Intentional About Your Community and Friendships

Now that we've talked about the types of people that are part of your community, let's assess your current community and feeling of belonging. Do you feel you have an optimal community of support around you? If you do, amazing! If you don't, you are not stuck here! To a large degree, you can choose your community.

When you are being intentional about your community, whether you're starting from scratch or assessing your current closest humans, it is so incredibly important to have friends who are helpful to your family and supportive of what you do. If someone isn't supportive of you and what you're trying to accomplish in life, it's time to make some decisions about who you spend your valuable, limited time and energy with.

To help you think about this, I invite you to spend some time mulling over the following questions:

- What qualities do you need in the people supporting you?

- What kinds of people fill your cup and create calm, and why?

- What kinds of people deplete you and cause chaos?

To build peace and calm into your life and start enjoying it more, you need to cut out elements that don't serve you, specifically the humans who disrupt and prevent calm (sorry, you can't do that with your kids, but they only disrupt you sometimes, right?). This will give you more flexibility to make mindful decisions about who you invite into your life in terms of friendships. (Breaking up with family is not always a possibility, but you *can* distance yourself.) This may sound like a harsh concept, but it's *not* selfish to distance yourself or terminate a friendship. It's okay that you and that friend aren't in alignment. Chances are they probably feel that way, too. And distancing doesn't have to be forever, because everyone evolves and grows. With limited energy and time, be selective of who you choose to spend your time with. Spend it with those who will fill you up and not drain you.

Letting go of a friendship, especially one you've had for many years, is no easy feat. It's a lot easier to say, and much harder to actually do it. As someone who is all about human connection, both personally and professionally, I know it's challenging to purposefully distance myself from someone, especially if it seems like they need help.

But here's the thing. *Other people aren't your responsibility* (except your kids, of course!). Other people are on their own journey, just as you are on yours. You are not their therapist or their parent. You are not obligated to be a sounding board at all hours, or deplete yourself and your calm in the process. Even if you can't cut someone out of your life completely, you *can* make changes to how you respond to those people to decrease the stressful effect they have on you.

Building my community (especially when I started anew after moving to San Francisco) and ensuring I had the right humans around me is an area I've worked on a lot as I've refined my *Chaos to Calm* strategies. Even though I am versed in psychology and human behavior, it was difficult for me to have a clear vision of who added to my life and who took from it, who added to my day-to-day energy, and who was an energy leech.

As a born nurturer and helper, I always want to be there for all beings, loved ones as well as strangers. It's definitely proved to be a problem at times. Learning how to distance and disconnect from those who don't serve in my life has been the hardest strategy I've had to learn, as it goes against my nature. I had to figure out how to keep my giving nature while not giving everything I had to someone who wasn't able or willing to give to me or acknowledge my giving as well.

In friendships with a history of love and depth, but that are taking too much of your time and energy, you can choose to spend less time and energy on them. You can see them less frequently, or only in certain situations, like in group settings. You can catch up occasionally rather than constantly. You don't need to put forth the concerted effort to stay connected to someone who 1) doesn't make the same effort to stay connected to you, 2) doesn't add benefit to your life, and 3) takes advantage of your generosity, kindness, availability, and giving energy.

In toxic friendships, ask yourself, "What does this relationship mean to me? Is it meaningful?" When you notice you're not your best self around that person, cut ties if possible, or minimize ties as a necessity. When you work hard to create the emotional space and time for peace, joy, and the things you love and want in your life, who do you want there with you? You're spending all this time and energy to create a calm and peaceful existence for yourself, and you need to find the right humans to share that space with you.

Another great way to evaluate whether your friendship is worth keeping is to ask yourself, if you were to meet them under a different context, would you intentionally choose to spend time with them and create and nurture that friendship? Be honest with yourself, because it could make or break your stress—is this friendship serving your life where you are *now*, not where you were decades or even a year ago? If you went on a "first date" with each of the humans closest to you, would you be a good match now?

How to Create Some Distance

If you find you need to back away from a friendship that is not serving you, remember that you are not at anyone's beck and call, and you can schedule a time to connect with each other. Make sure there's an end time so you can leave gracefully, which is harder when it's open-ended. Have more group hangouts so you don't have to be one-on-one with that person. If it's someone you see all the time naturally (at your kid's school, workplace, local coffee shop, etc.), tell them you're going through a life transition and it's going to be a bit before you can hang out. When they reach out to you, whether by phone, email, or text, don't feel obligated to respond right away, though when you do, don't leave it open-ended by asking a question. You can absolutely write, "Thinking of you," but don't ask, "How are you?" Naturally your friend will become more distant when they find they are not getting what they want from you. Most likely they will find someone else to fill that space. The friendship can naturally dissolve.

You don't have to ghost anyone—never do that. Instead, simply reduce your communications, and reduce the amount of time spent together. If they notice you're not responding, they may ask what's up. You can respond by saying something like, "There's been a lot going on lately and I've been needing to prioritize my time and energy," or "I care about you and I just don't have as much energy and time to connect as often."

YOUR TURN

The goal of this exercise is to pare down your community to be just the people who meet your criteria for calm; you'll decide who you want to be close with now, regardless of past history. This is the time to put all obligatory feelings aside. Rate your community purely on an objective scale, based on the relationships that fill you and give you calm and those that detract from it.

Realize that friendships are yin and yang—there will be times you'll need more from your friendships and times your friends will need more from you. If there is a pattern or trend of your friend needing so much that it's getting in the way of you being able to show up for your responsibilities and priorities, and it's begun to affect your calm, you will have to determine whether it's a toxic relationship or just a moment in time.

In trying to build a life of calm, you need to make courageous decisions.

- [ ] Make a list of the people who you interact with the most in your life, besides your kids and spouse. These are the people you either talk to regularly (daily, weekly, monthly, no matter the method—in person, text, phone, FaceTime). Include family, friends, coworkers, people who live in your home besides the kids and your partner, people you spend time with in the office, and people you interact with in between home and work. Literally, list anyone you interact with regularly.
- [ ] Circle the people who fill your cup the most.

- Does this person fill your cup?
- Does this person leave you feeling better than you were before?
- Does this person hear you?
- Does this person support you?
- Does this person add to your life?
- Does this person increase your energy?
- Does this person lift you up?

☐ Circle the name of each person you would give a consistent yes.

☐ Put a dash next to the names of the people you feel you need to limit in your life.

☐ Put an X next to the names of people you need to break up with.

☐ Circled list: Write them a note and tell them how much they mean to you and why. "I am so grateful for your friendship—I can be myself with you and I love that we found each other." "Thank you for listening when I was having a hard morning. It meant a lot to me."

☐ Dash and X (distance or breakup) list: Begin implementing the advice from above that feels right to you (spend less time, have a direct conversation, or set boundaries).

☐ Weed the initial list down to only the people who meet the *Chaos to Calm* criteria. Keep only the ones who most often bring you joy, fill you up, give you energy, lift up your life, facilitate peace, and support your family and your dreams).

Keep in mind that there are circumstances when you will be forced to give more than you get (like commiting to caregiving), and there are ways to find peace in that by changing expectations. Be realistic about what that particular relationship entails. You can reevaluate your expectations and adjust later if the reality doesn't meet what you originally thought it would be like.

How to Attract and Build Your Community

If you're finding there aren't many entries on your weeded-down list, don't despair! I didn't have any when I first moved to the Bay Area (except my friends back in LA, of course!). All it means is that you have an opportunity to start fresh with who you bring into your life. Ideally, it would be great if you had a couple of every type of community friend, but truly, one person is all you need. A partner, a sibling, a childhood friend, a brand-new friend, your person.

Here are my favorite tips to help develop a community:

Be open and communicate your needs. Share what's going on for you. One time I shared with a parent I didn't know well that Kyle was out of town for work for nine days. She offered to host a playdate for Sage and her son and I gladly accepted!

Allow for help. People want to help. Accepting their help allows for you to participate in the virtuous circle of asking for and giving help.

Do things of interest to you. This is a great way to meet like-minded people.

Join a group. For example, Hey Mama for entrepreneurs, AA, specialized Facebook groups (e.g., the breastfeeding group that saved me), book clubs, religious settings, hiking meetups. You don't have to know every group member personally to feel you belong.

Say hello. Ask for other people's names and introduce yourself. When Kyle and I first moved, we found a delicious restaurant near home. We met the owner, who was also our server, and told him we were new to town. We got to talking and the next time we went to that restaurant, he remembered us, (and even remembered our drink order!), and we saw him around town, too.

Be proactive. Invite over a family or friend you don't know well but want to. I once took a risk and invited a new family at school for Thanksgiving, and we ended up being great support families for each other.

OWN YOUR CALM: COMMUNITY RECAP

Having a community is imperative to calm because it is human nature to need others in a give-and-take fashion, as well as to support you when you need help. A strong community gives you a sense of belonging and peace of mind; you are not in this world alone.

- ✓ Not everyone has to be your best friend. Friends can be deep, long-term, short-term, contextual, or helper friends who help each other out but aren't deeply close.

- ✓ Assess your community and lean away from those who don't help your calm and lean into those who do.

- ✓ To build a community if you don't have one, begin extending invitations to people you think you might like, join like-minded hobby groups, volunteer, or join a group either in person or online.

nication

What to Say and How to Listen
to Get the Support You Need

"We are stronger when we listen,
and smarter when we share."

—RANIA AL ABDULLAH

YOU PROBABLY FEEL LIKE ALL you do is communicate. You're constantly directing the kids each day. Making appointments. Calling in absences. Arranging trips. Running meetings at work. Talking to clients and customers. Discussing weekend plans. Asking for or giving advice to friends. Fielding endless calls from your stalker, Spam Likely.

You may be talking a lot, but are you truly communicating? Are you repeating yourself a lot? Do you feel like you have to explain yourself over and over? You can save a lot of time and frustration (and increase your calm) by refining your communication skills. Being an effective communicator is a critical *Chaos to Calm* skill.

Effective Communication Directly Affects Calm

Effective Communication Is a Two-Way Street.

Communication consists of two parts: expressing yourself *and* listening to others. Communicating isn't only about getting *your* ideas and concepts heard and acted upon; it also requires that you listen, understand, and take action on what *other* people say. This is called *active listening* and if you do it right, you'll find that effective communication is less about talking and more about listening. Active listening means not just understanding the words or the information being communicated, but also understanding the *emotions* and *intentions* behind what you hear. Being an effective communicator (we'll get to that shortly) helps the person listening to you understand not only what you're saying, but also *why* you're saying it and what you truly mean.

Types of Communication

When you consider the many ways you communicate in a day, you probably think about making a call, texting, chatting in person, or emailing. Those are all modes of communication and they can be bucketed in different communication types, including verbal, nonverbal (written and body language), visual, formal, informal, in person, virtual, and listening. In the nonverbal category, there's also body language, including facial expressions. Think of those times you give your kids that "Mom is so serious right now you better knock that off" face. No words are needed, right? Or the look of pride your kiddo sees when they spot you in the audience during their Three Little Pigs play. A lot can be said with a simple glance, turn of cheek, or the rise of a middle finger when someone cuts you off.

Speaking with someone face-to-face, either in person or virtually, would be categorized as verbal *and* nonverbal, as there are words coming out of your mouth (verbal), but there is also your body language, tone of voice, facial expressions, and gestures (all nonverbal). Texting, emailing, and online messaging are all written communication, and they land somewhere between formal and informal depending on who your recipient is. Emojis can say a lot! I love me some good emojis. The key methods of communication that I'll refer to throughout this chapter to increase calm are verbal, nonverbal (body language and written), and listening.

Effective communication is a key element for calm, as calm is more easily achieved when you feel like you are able to be heard and understood. Additionally, when you're able to hear and understand others, it's easier to be calm with those around you.

Imagine your five-year-old just yelled at you. Your reflexive reaction may be to scream back, "Stop yelling!" However, a five-year-old is going to respond better if you explain that when she yells:

- She won't get her way by yelling,

- It makes you feel upset and sad, and

- Talking in a more gentle voice means that you can hear and understand her.

With communication like this, your child will be more receptive to your intervention and will most likely stop yelling in order to communicate with you than if you screamed back at her. An effective communicative approach such as this means everyone ends up in a much calmer state. Over time, and with enough repetition (these are kids, after all; it's never one and done.), your child's behavior will change. So look forward to more calm speaking and less yelling in your future!

Through effective communication, you'll be able to better understand and be understood by those around you. This naturally will lead to you getting more support for the things that are important to you. When people understand what your needs are, and you are clear on others' needs, there is space for harmony and compassion. With understanding and compassion, people are more likely to provide support, rally with you, and create space for your needs.

Practicing effective communication builds trust and respect. It's a whole lot easier to talk to your partner when there's trust, honesty, and respect between you, rather than resentment, anger, and ego. When communicating effectively, your partner will be confident in knowing and understanding your needs.

Listening Is a Superpower

Listening is one of the most important skills a human can master. At a minimum, being a good listener builds and strengthens relationships of all kinds and in all contexts. Listening is fundamental when engaging and communicating, as it helps you better understand the world around you and others' experiences and perspectives, and it provides a sense of grounding and connectedness.

When someone feels heard and understood, they feel safe and are more likely to be vulnerable and share openly. This allows you to be able to truly understand who they are, where they're coming from, and why they behave a certain way and make the choices they do. In turn, you won't have to guess how they're doing or feel out of touch, and you can bask in calm, knowing your relationships are all safe and sound.

Think about a time when you've been listened to. Doesn't it feel great when someone makes eye contact with you while you share what's on your mind and in your heart? And don't you feel so much lighter after you share something with someone who is truly listening? Even when the person you're talking to says nothing, you feel seen, heard, and understood. Sometimes you feel that *especially* when they say nothing. When this beautiful moment happens, you feel connected. Even to a stranger!

Once, while I was ordering coffee, the barista asked how my morning was going. I responded honestly (not what she was expecting!), saying it had been a rough morning. The kids had been particularly challenging, I didn't sleep well (although that's all the time—yay kids), there was a huge mess in the kitchen, and three loads of laundry were waiting for me when I got home at the end of the day. The barista looked me in the eye, smiled, and said, "You got this." I had no idea who she was, but I felt connected and grateful to her at that moment. Thank you, barista, for holding space for me!

How Listening Promotes Calm

When you make the effort to listen to someone, they'll notice that you are interested. If you aren't fully present in a conversation and are distracted (looking at your phone, playing a game, searching, texting, internally perseverating on a problem), the other person can feel it, and they'll stop sharing. They won't trust that you respect their thoughts and feelings. We've all been there. The more you practice active listening, the more goodwill you'll build, and the next time you need to be deeply heard, you'll find that people are more likely to truly be there for you.

One time my daughter Leya was telling me about some goings-on at school and my phone blew up with email notifications. I looked at my phone and got hooked by a work email that needed immediate attention. I looked back up to apologize to her for picking up my phone and realized she had left the room. I went to find her, and asked if she would continue her story, and she responded with, "It doesn't matter." Oh man, did I feel terrible.

Listening increases empathy because you'll understand the world more deeply and thoroughly. By being completely present in the moment and fully listening, you can hear different perspectives, backgrounds, and experiences without layering filters of your own experiences and biases. Actively listening, without being distracted or focused on what *you* want to say next, creates the opportunity for curiosity. When listening directly to the source, with an open heart and mind,

130

without your assumptions getting in the way, you gain a deeper under-standing of other perspectives as well as empathy and compassion. It's so much easier to be calm when you can empathize with someone, even if you disagree.

My friend Tabitha and I decided to meet for a margarita. I showed up on time (I had hit traffic but had my calendar cushion—yay me!). Tabitha had a history of being late, which irked me, but she was a dear friend and I always left our meetings feeling empowered and happy. This particular time, twenty minutes went by (and a 16-ounce margarita went down). Still no sign, no text. Annoyed, I called her on the phone as if it were 1992. Tabitha's hello revealed she'd been crying. She had been visiting her aunt with Alzheimer's, and her aunt had forgotten her name for the first time. Having had experience with chronically ailing loved ones, I immediately became empathetic, and it diffused any frustration I'd had. She told me she was on her way, and I ordered her favorite drink and met her with a hug when she arrived.

Positive relationships of all kinds are built on the back of respect. Listening provides a space for judgment-free sharing that is safe and open. If a relationship is strained, listening can help get the relationship back on track. This is true with friendships, partnerships, spouses, chil-dren, family, and colleagues. Effective listening will make a strong rela-tionship even stronger.

Recently I was on the phone with an old friend, Sarah. Sarah is the type of person who interrupts whatever is being said anytime she feels her kid or animal needs correcting. Whenever I called her I never felt like she was listening to what I was saying, because as soon as I'd say, "What would you do if . . ." she'd scream out, "Henry! Stop barking!" Finally, I decided to bring it up with her, as it was affecting my desire to keep in touch. "Sarah, when would be a good time to talk to you about some-thing on my mind? I would appreciate it if you could do it at a time when you had no distractions." I asked. Sarah then made arrangements for private, uninterrupted time and when I called, she listened to my heart as I explained that I really wanted to keep in touch but found our conversations were more filled with overhearing discipline than true sharing. Together we came up with a plan to have our catch-up calls be at a location and time that was less distracting for her.

When people aren't listening to each other, it's easy to misinterpret what's being said. Misunderstandings aren't always a big deal with huge repercussions or consequences, but even a bunch of small ones over time cause trust to break down and lead to bigger problems.. Something as simple as misunderstanding the start time of a playdate, to something bigger, like roles and responsibilities of a work project, can really mess up good intentions. When you are truly listening, you can be calm, knowing that you fully understand what's going on, the expectations, your role, others' roles, and whatever else is needed.

My friend Sam shared that there was a new hire in marketing who was meant to be her peer on a project. The new coworker disagreed with Sam about the creative direction of their project, and Sam was pissed because she knew that the project would be a lot more successful if they went with her own suggestion. Sam became combative in their meetings and held a grudge because her coworker wanted to go in a different direction.

When Sam told me about how frustrated she was, I asked her if she had asked her coworker any questions about why she wanted to go in that direction, and Sam hadn't. I told Sam that she might benefit from asking her coworker what she imagined the outcome would be, and how it would benefit the business. When she did, it came out that her coworker was missing some important information about the project and its objectives because she was new to the company, which was understandable. Sam clarified the project and shared some past experiences she had learned from. They moved forward with Sam's idea and resolved their working relationship.

Often, people think they're adding value by offering information and talking a lot. But being engaged by talking is not the same as really hearing what's happening, asking the right questions, and gaining a deep understanding of the situation. With real listening, everyone can be on the same page, be more effective with their responsibilities and tasks, minimize misunderstandings, and save time. Who knew you could gain so much simply by listening?

Active Listening

Now that you know why listening is a much-needed skill, let's go over how to do it right. Active listening means to focus completely on the person speaking, understand their message, comprehend and integrate the information, and respond thoughtfully.

In order to actively listen, you *must* make a conscious effort to not just *hear* what someone is saying but to also *really absorb it*—to digest the information and truly understand.

Now that you are thoroughly convinced that active listening is going to bring a ton of calm to your world, here's how to do it.

Show You're Listening

1. Turn your body to face the person talking to you.

2. Make and maintain eye contact.

3. Notice nonverbal signals, such as facial expressions and body language. All of this is a part of the conversation and the information they're telling you. Are they tense? Open and loose? Are their arms crossed defensively? Are they rubbing their eyes as if they're tired or upset?

4. Don't impose your opinions or go immediately into problem-solving mode unless invited to do so. The person you are listening to may not be ready for your solutions or ideas yet and rather just want a supportive ear. Holding space by listening can be much

more rewarding for the speaker than giving them advice. If they want advice, you can pretty much bet they'll ask you for it. If you have a brilliant idea that you must share, ask if they want to hear it before just blurting it out. Say, "I have an idea, would you like to hear it?"

5. Nod your head, smile, and make affirming noises, like "yes" and "uh huh." It sounds small, but doing these things shows you're listening and encourages the speaker to continue.

Be Present

Make eye contact. Don't look at your watch or phone (place your phone facedown if needed). Try to refrain from fidgeting or playing with your hair or fingers.

Eliminate distractions. If you can, silence your phone or even turn it off. If you're on a video conference call, don't try to check your email or play a game. You'll lose focus and the speaker will pick up on it.

Pay attention. Don't plan what you're going to say next while someone is speaking. If your attention is on what you're going to say, you aren't fully able to hear what is being said.

Take notes. In more elaborate discussions, if you want to take notes, tell or ask the person if you can take notes.

If you notice a distraction, return to listening. If you do get distracted, like the doorbell rings during a call or your kid melts down, notice the distraction and come straight back to listening. If your phone dings, and you have to look at it because it's your kids' school, openly say why. "Can you give me a moment? It's the kids' school; just making sure it's not urgent." It's helpful to also set the stage before a conversation if you know you may be interrupted. For example, if you know groceries will likely be delivered while you are on a call or a visit, tell the person the interruption might happen and why, so it's not jarring or disrespectful. This way, you can gracefully handle it by pausing the conversation and then transition back.

Avoid drama dumping. I have a colleague with a teenage daughter and her friend group has an effective way to stay out of the drama dump that I think is brilliant. Before they text a dramatic situation or feeling (I mean, they're teenage girls!), they ask, "Is it a good time to talk to you about something heavy?" And if they need to vent, they clarify, "I just need to vent; feel free to respond later!" Go teen calm!

Don't interrupt. Allow the speaker to finish their thoughts to completion before you respond with your questions or thoughts.

Repeat back. Paraphrase the other person's words to make sure you heard them correctly and to validate their thoughts. You can say, "So what I'm hearing you say is _____. which makes you feel like _____." Or, "I want to make sure I understand _____ can you repeat _____?"

Ask questions. To show you are engaged and to clarify meaning, you might ask something like, "What do you mean when you say _____?"

Be Curious

Ask open-ended questions. Seek first to understand instead of to be understood. By showing curiosity and interest in the other person's perspective, you gain their trust and they will share more honestly. Even if the subject matter is boring or offensive to you, keep in mind that you can *always* be interested by being curious, supporting the other person, learning something new, and being open-minded.

Don't Judge

You can't be empathetic if you're judging someone as they're talking, even silently. Making judgmental statements or judgy body language motions (like eye-rolling, dismissive hand-waving) will stop the other person from sharing. Extend respect, compassion, grace, and forgiveness to the degree that you would like it extended to you.

Even if you disagree, keep an open mind and approach the conversation with curiosity. You can ask questions like, "Oh, that's really interesting, what made you think/feel that way?"

Real Listening in Action

You know how you feel compelled to say, "Hey, how was your day?" as soon as your kids or partner comes through the door? You're probably mid-task, and not really in a place to truly listen to the answer, but you ask anyway. My advice to you is this: Don't ask unless you're ready to listen. Shout out a "Hi, welcome home, I want to hear about your day when I finish cutting the gum out of your sister's hair." Save further conversation until you have *your* stuff done (or you're at a good stopping point), so you can be present when other people need to tell you *their* stuff.

Raise your hand if you feel like everyone interrupts you to tell you sh*t ALL THE TIME! Me, me! As parents, we're interrupted and requested—demanded, even—to *watch* (how many times do we hear "Mom, watch me do this!" in a day?), *listen* (our kids blurt out what's on their minds constantly, which is totally normal), and *do* ("Mom, I'm huuungggggrrry!") constantly. But when your child is telling you about drama with their friends, and you're half tuning them out because you're mid-work email, you're not really listening to them. When you try to listen at a time that's not good for you, it'll lead to you resenting the interruptor, when it's up to you to set a boundary on listening (in nonemergency situations, of course!).

It's a child's job to get your attention—they don't have the self-control and analytical skills adults do to time their requests at good moments. It's up to you to set healthy boundaries.

The thing is, even while you may be getting requests all the time, you can lovingly set boundaries for yourself so you don't have to drop everything you're doing every time someone needs something from you. This includes your parents, your partner, your friends, your kids, anyone. Here are more ideas of things to say in a moment when it's not a good time for you to listen: "I can tell how excited you are to tell me about what just happened; just give me X time to finish what I'm doing and then you'll have my full attention. I'm excited to hear it soon" or "I want to help you with this issue so much, and I'll be able to focus on it at xyz time."

You get the idea. Lots of great things happen that will increase your calm when you get in this pattern:

- You will be able to give way better responses to the other person because you'll be more thoughtful and not distracted, resentful, and stressed.

- The other person will really *feel* your attention, and they'll feel special, loved, and important.

- Your household will get used to you not being immediately available to hear all of their stuff at any moment of the day. They'll learn to observe you before interrupting you, and the less they interrupt, the better for your peace and sanity! (Yes, it will take time for your household to adjust, but with enough repetition and reinforcement, success will be yours!)

LEONA
the listener

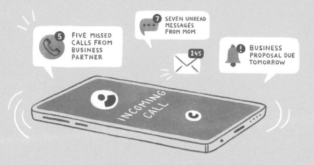

Leona was a small-business owner, wife, and mother of two energetic sons. Her days were long and exhausting. She worked from the moment she woke up to the moment she laid her head down at night. Leona was the sole breadwinner of her family and felt immense pressure to make sure her business was successful, or her family wouldn't have enough money to pay the bills.

Overwhelming stress ate at her, and she found herself responding to emails and checking her phone constantly to try to keep up. She was always distracted during family time, which turned into such a habit that her marriage started to suffer. Her husband and sons stopped talking to her about their days, because whenever they started talking to her she'd check her phone to see what she was missing. This made them feel ignored. Although she felt awful not being present for her family and more involved in the day-to-day, she also had conflicting feelings because of business demands and financial responsibilities.

Leona and I talked at length about the right approach to improve her relationships without sacrificing the time she needed to devote to her business. She started practicing active listening, and when she communicated *when* she'd be able to listen, her home life improved dramatically.

Leona also created a new boundary at dinnertime by leaving her phone on the kitchen counter and putting it on silent mode so she wouldn't get distracted or compelled to check messages every time she heard a ping.

Leona practiced saying to her kids, "I want to hear all about your day. I just need two minutes to finish this email and then I will give you my full attention." And she followed through by actually doing it. With her husband, Leona told him she wanted to make sure that they had ten minutes each day to connect just the two of them, and she would actively listen as he told her about his daily happenings and vice versa.

Leona apologized to her family (an act of courage we should all do more often, as taking accountability for our actions also builds trust) for not having given her full attention in the past. She said she was going to practice communicating when she was unavailable because she was in the middle of something important for work and she would tell them when she'd be available and ready to give them her full attention. Leona also practiced active listening by making affirming noises while they spoke, making eye contact, paraphrasing back what she heard, and asking questions.

Her boys now are so excited to tell her about their days and her relationship with her husband has improved dramatically! Leona achieved more calm in her life by knowing she was addressing everyone's needs—including her own!—and, by example, she taught her children how to do the same.

YOUR TURN

Plan for when you have to say, "Not now."

- [ ] The next time a kid, friend, partner, or colleague interrupts my flow with a request to listen, and I'm not fully present, I will say this: _____.

Getting Heard

We've all found ourselves asking for help and feeling like no one is listening. One of the biggest killers of calm is when we have *so much* to do, and although we take the time to ask for support on *one* thing, it still doesn't get done. So frustrating!

In this section, I'll show you the best communication tips that have worked for me and my clients, which will help you get the support you need.

Be Proactive vs. Reactive

Planning ahead versus reacting to a crisis will help you maintain your calm and reduce stress. When a challenging situation comes up, and you feel there wasn't time to prepare before having to handle it, you can still maintain a proactive state by taking a moment to think, breathe, and *then* respond instead of having a knee-jerk reaction, which often results in increased stress and a poor outcome.

When you take a moment before responding, you can actively calm down any harmful adrenaline and decrease your body's stress response to get to a calmer state. From that calmer state, you can respond more thoughtfully. Giving yourself time to be mindful brings calm to you and others in the situation.

BE PROACTIVE ABOUT GETTING DIRECT HELP

When you know you'll need support, give as much notice as possible to those you'll need help from. Keep in mind the help you need could be anything from direct help (asking someone to pick up your kid after school) to indirect assistance (extending grace and understanding if you're not as responsive as usual).

Communicate *what* you have going on, *the specific help* you think you'll need, and *why* you need that help. The why is important here so the other person can feel empathy toward your situation and be even more motivated to help. Respect their needs as well—ask whether they can do it and whether they need anything to make sure that all goes smoothly. Send them reminders leading up to the event you need help with, which can ensure smooth support (if the other person finds that helpful).

It's a lot easier to get support where you need it *before* the event versus during the need. For example, if you know in the late afternoon you'll need help after dinner, you can express to your partner, "I have so much to do before bed tonight. I have about a dozen emails to respond to and eight customer orders to fulfill. And there is laundry to be folded as well. What are your plans after dinner? Would you be able to help fold the laundry, so I don't need to go to bed so late?" I promise this will work a lot better than if, after dinner, you say in mid-martyr meltdown, "Ugh, I have so much to do! I don't know how I'm ever going to get this all done without going to bed after midnight. I feel like I have to do everything around here!" and expect your partner to know what to do and jump in at the last minute.

Planning ahead respects your family and community's needs. If you have a big deadline at work, you can ask for help with picking up the kids like this: "I have to finish this project in two weeks and need all the time I can get. Would you be able to pick up the kids after school this week so that I can get some extra time to work?" Being proactive versus reactionary isn't just for the sake of others; it's for your sanity, too. Knowing you'll have the support you need ahead of time will increase your calm.

Appointments are a key example of being proactive where it counts. There are certain appointments and events that show up at regular intervals (weekly, yearly). If you schedule your annual physical at the same time every year, you can create your list of questions leading up to the appointment instead of only seeing the doctor when something is off and you need to go in urgently. Make teeth cleanings every six months instead of when you feel a pain in your molar. Schedule your hair appointments before you know your roots are going to grow out. It's a lot easier to get appointments when you schedule them in advance rather than when you need them urgently, and you'll have a sense of calm knowing your appointments are all lined up.

BE PROACTIVE ABOUT GETTING INDIRECT HELP

When you're going through a transition or a period of time when you know you won't be able to be as responsive as usual, take a proactive stance with your relationships as a way to foster calm. For example, if you have a huge deliverable at work, are training for a marathon, having a baby, moving, lost a loved one, or a child is in crisis, everyone will benefit from your strategic communication to set expectations on how responsive you can be. For example, if you're having a baby, text your friends before the baby's born and tell them they may not hear from you as quickly as usual because you need a few months to acclimate to motherhood.

If you want to focus more on *Chaos to Calm* techniques, let everyone know you've embarked on a personal journey and need a lot of time for self-reflection. Make sure they're aware that if you don't reply right away, it's not personal. You'll reply when you can. So often, especially for us women, we drop everything to be there for a friend. Certainly that is kind and generous and a good thing to do. We need people to drop everything for us too sometimes. When I proactively let my friends know what I'm going through or training for, their feelings aren't hurt when they don't hear back from me immediately, and then calm ensues. This has worked for me time and time again.

In fact, while I was writing this book, I proactively told many people in my world that I would need to postpone coffee dates and catch-ups to focus on writing as much as possible. And when someone I hadn't told reached out, I transparently shared that I was head-down until the book was done and that I would reach out when I had finished and had more time again. Most of the time, people's reactions—if they are genuine friends (see Community on page 100 to help you figure out who is a true friend)—are completely supportive and understanding.

Still, sometimes, there will be people who come off as mad, aggressive, disappointed, and unsupportive. Nine times out of ten, I've come to realize that their intention is not malicious. They are simply responding to their environment. They either have a strong defense mechanism or they have their guard up because of distress they are experiencing or have experienced. They may lash out if you're not responsive because a different friend or someone else important to them may have hurt them in the past. Start by presuming positive intent (the next topic)—it'll help you handle that kind of human behavior in a less stressful and more constructive way.

Presume Positive Intent

Everyone's doing the best they can—yes, even your nosy mother-in-law—and if you remember that in your heart, you'll see the world much more calmly and positively.

Assuming positive intent means that when you're on the receiving end of a negative action or behavior, instead of assuming that the doer (or neglector) is a thoughtless jerk, redirect your thoughts to presume that their actions were done with no ill intent. For example, maybe a truck cuts you off on the freeway. Your instinctive reaction is probably shaking your fist and yelling, "What a jackass! He almost ran us off the road!" But you *could* choose to think, "He may have had an emergency and needs to get to his destination quickly." Or, "Wow, he must be late for something very important and obviously needs to get there very quickly." Of course, it could be he's just a total jerk-wad, in which case, finding the funny in the situation is always a good coping mechanism.

When you assume positive intent, especially with those closest to you, they'll feel your positivity and openness, which will facilitate a supportive relationship. People are more willing to help and support you when they experience you as a positive and open-minded person.

Here Are More Positive Intent Reframes:

Situation: *Your partner lets the kids be on screens for hours, and you disagree with this adamantly and it sends you into a rage (not calm!).*

Negative Assumption: He's so lazy and doesn't want to spend quality time with his own kids!

Positive Assumption: Maybe he's going through a difficult moment (no judging what that is) and really needed the kids to be entertained.

Calm Action: Ask from a place of calm what's going on and how you can support him. If this is a common occurrence, ask to brainstorm other ways that the kids can be occupied without screens, like scheduling play-dates or visits with the grandparents.

Situation: *Your colleague is late to deliver their portion of a project.*

Negative Assumption: Ugh, she has the worst time management skills! How did she even get this job? Does she think I have time to do it all?

Positive Assumption: I hope she's okay. Maybe she had a family emergency or health issue that prevented her from being able to complete her work on time.

Calm Action: Approach her and share that you noticed she's been behind on her deliverables. You can ask if everything is okay and whether there's anything she needs to get back on track.

Situation: *Your teenager asks, "Why are you wearing that?"*

Negative Assumption: Oh my god, I look like a fool and my teen is so embarrassed by me. I should change!

Positive Assumption: Maybe they're not judging my fashion sense, maybe they think I'm just at home today, and they don't know I'm having lunch with an old friend.

Calm Action: Respond with, "I love this dress and haven't worn it in forever." And then, if you want to actually know the answer, you can ask, "Why do you ask?"

In the absence of information (maybe their communication skills of proactively letting you know what's going on aren't as honed as yours will be now), it's beneficial for your calm to assume the best in people. So often we assume the worst in others, and when we do that, we bring unnecessary stress on ourselves. And when you presume that others are coming from a place of kindness and positivity, you'll be able to keep anxious thoughts at bay and create calm.

Understanding Love Languages

You may have heard of the love languages created by Gary Chapman, in his book, *The Five Love Languages: How to Express Heartfelt Commitment to Your Mate*. In a nutshell, your love language is the way you most feel and receive love.

While love languages work wonders in romantic relationships, they can also help in any of your close relationships. Knowing another person's love language allows you to show your love and appreciation for them in the exact way they'll feel it most (and not waste time doing things that may not resonate). Bonus: By knowing and sharing your love language, it can help those around you show you *their* love and appreciation in the way you feel it most, too.

Here are the love languages expressed in Chapman's book; which one resonates with you most?

Physical Touch—You feel loved the most when your partner stops you for a hug in the hallway or makes out with you while you're in the middle of emptying the dishwasher. Non-romantically, you feel loved when a friend touches your arm while telling you a story or thanking you for a gift.

Words of Affirmation—You feel loved the most when your partner tells you they love you, leaves love notes for you on the bathroom mirror, tells you that they appreciate you, or gives you compliments. Non-romantically, you feel loved when a colleague tells you how impactful your work is or sends you an email thanking you for going above and beyond.

Acts of Service—You feel loved the most when your partner does things for you that help you or make your life easier. Maybe they run your car through the car wash, make dinner when you're tired, or put a glass of water at your bedside before you go to bed. Non-romantically, you feel cared about when your friend asks if they can bring your kid home from school when you have an especially full day or if they can get you anything from the grocery store while they are there.

Quality Time—You feel loved the most when your partner gives you their time and attention, when you do something with your partner you both enjoy, and when you can share an experience and create a memory together. These activities could be date nights, going on a hike together, or playing a game together. Even doing chores together could count as quality time if you're really present with each other while you are doing it. Non-romantically, you feel loved when your coworkers take you out for a birthday meal or your sibling invites you to the beach.

Receiving Gifts—You feel loved the most when your partner gets you gifts or treats they know you'd love. You'd probably get turned on if your partner noticed your earbuds were broken and replaced them for you or left you a box of Junior Mints on your desk because they're your favorite candy. Non-romantically, you feel loved when your friend brings you a bagel and a coffee knowing you have a busy day ahead, or your boss sends you a bottle of wine, thanking you for your hard work at the end of the quarter. This doesn't mean you're materialistic; it's truly the thought that counts.

Your Partner's Love Language

The first thing to do on the love language list is to get fluent in how to show and receive love from your partner. You know, the one you chose to live life and raise children with. The one who is your main person in this game of tag called partnership and parenting. Your goal is to foster love and appreciation of your partner through good communication. When you have a healthy, loving, and appreciative relationship, every other facet of life falls more easily into place. When "love is grand" all else seems rosier, doesn't it?

Knowing your partner's love language will increase your calm, because when you're both coming from a place of appreciation and love, you'll naturally want to help do whatever it takes for the other to be happy more often.

Love Languages in Practice

My husband's main love languages are physical touch and words. I know that he feels loved when I reach for his hand when we are in the grocery store, when I cuddle up on the couch with him after the kids are in bed, or when I stick a Post-it to the bathroom mirror telling him how handsome he is. My main love languages are quality time and acts of service. Knowing this, Kyle will ask Leya and Miya to babysit the boys periodically so we can have a date night at our favorite local margarita lounge.

Once you have the key to your partner's love language, you can use it to resolve conflicts more quickly and add more peace and calm to your life. When Kyle and I are in a pickle, we know snuggling (his love language) and quality time (my love language) will cool us off. Or if I'm in a moment of stress with a deadline or I'm super low on energy and feeling the need to be a hermit, Kyle knows the best way to help me is to do an act of service, such as taking over dinner duty to give me the gift of time. Or he'll leave a Post-it note on my laptop with a heart.

Conversely, when I make breakfast for myself, I make extra for Kyle and squeeze his shoulder as I put it on his desk while he's on a work call. It takes such little effort and time for me to do this because I'm already making it, and it makes him feel cared for. Revved up with love, guess who is more willing to make sure I get some child-free time for a little at-home pampering? (Oh how I love a nice face mask and quiet reading session.)

Others' Love Languages

Knowing the quickest route to the hearts of your kids, colleagues, and even your manager will make resolving conflict or maintaining a positive relationship easier.

Want a smoother relationship with your parents, siblings, or in-laws? Know what makes them feel appreciated and create goodwill by paying attention to their love language. This will come back to you tenfold in support. For example, if your mom watches the kids a couple of days a week for free (lucky you!) and her love language is gifts, you could give her a favorite bottle of wine or a book you think she'd like as a thank you. If words make your father-in-law feel special, a simple "I really appreciate how you always support the kids" goes a long way. Or to your sister-in-law, "You always have the kids' favorite snacks in your pantry. They love spending time with you. I'm so grateful for your thoughtfulness."

Do your kids feel the most loved when you praise them verbally, or take them out for some quality time like getting boba together? Maybe it's acts of service, like emptying the dishwasher for them when it's their turn on the chore wheel. Or perhaps it's touch, when you can take a few minutes to snuggle with them. Take opportunities, even for no reason at all (sometimes that's the most impactful time), to fill up their love meter and watch how it changes the dynamic between you. Instead of them constantly nagging or pestering you for this and that thing, they will feel more content (and give you more peace!).

My mother's love language is quality time. Being that she lives in Los Angeles while I'm in San Francisco, it's hard to spend regular time together. But one thing I can count on is that she'll come visit whenever she gets the chance. And when we go visit her, she makes sure she's completely present for us. She takes the kids to theme parks, treats them to ice cream, and watches movies on the couch with all of us snuggled around her.

If you know your boss has a heavy week ahead and is a gift person, drop off a coffee in the morning or a bar of chocolate in the afternoon. It's not being a kiss-ass to be nice. Just hand it over and say, "I thought you could use this today." When you foster goodwill with your boss, they may be more inclined to share important company info with you or be more understanding when you need time off. When your boss knows you appreciate them, it makes for a calmer work environment. And in an environment with good mojo, you'll get tasks done more efficiently. If you're a boss, it's helpful to know the love languages of your team members so you can tap into what keeps each person most motivated. (Of course, probably not including the love language of touch. We don't want to inadvertently bring Human Resource complaints into the picture here.)

When you know the fastest way to make someone feel better, stressful misinterpretations will decrease and any squabbles that might arise will be quickly mended. For example, my kids' birth mom lives in another country, so not all love languages are available to her. She sends the kids gifts (her love language) throughout the year. If the kids aren't feeling her love at a particular moment, I will remind them that when she sends gifts it's her way of showing how much she's thinking of and loving them when she isn't physically there.

Knowing what boosts people around you and offering them little acts of love and kindness keeps you and them in a beautiful space and maintains positive relationships. And, with all that goodwill and positivity, when you need something like a hug or time alone, they're more inclined to give it to you because they're coming from a place of feeling loved and appreciated.

Now, I'm not saying to use love languages to manipulate everyone into getting what you need. Don't be an asshole. Or codependent. Utilizing love languages is about maintaining joy, happiness, and, say it with me, *calm*. If your loved ones are in a good flow, happy and feeling loved, *you'll* be more calm. You'll be more likely to find yourself taking a long bath peacefully while everyone's happily chilling. When everyone feels content and loved, they aren't constantly seeking that from you. It's all about being proactive.

Keep in mind that love languages can change. This is a great exercise to look at every year or so. Maybe you were more of a gift person in your early adulthood but now you're more appreciative of quality time or words of affirmation. As I've evolved over the course of my life, so have my love languages. The more types of love your kids are exposed to, the more they learn how to show their love to you and others. And they'll grow up having an organic and holistic approach to showing and receiving love.

GLORIA
the gifter

&

WILLIAM
the wordsmith

My client Gloria wanted to increase calm in her life. For our first session, I wanted to find out what the biggest chaos creators were. Gloria confided that her main source of stress had to do with not feeling appreciated or on the same page with her husband, William, whom she deeply loved.

Through some coaching, we found out that Gloria felt most loved when she got a thoughtful gift, and William felt the most appreciated when he was verbally praised.

We set up a plan to get them into a rising spiral of appreciation that would foster calm, fulfillment, and reciprocal help. Gloria set an alarm every afternoon to send William a special note, thanking him for a thoughtful action, expressing love, flirting, or making him feel like the stud she saw him as. She bought a set of beautiful note cards and in each one wrote one sentence of what she loved and appreciated about William. She put a card in various places where she knew William would find them. About once a week, he opened a sock drawer or the coffee maker, and there was a card! He opened up the medicine cabinet to get his shaving cream and propped up against the bottle—boom!—another card.

What Gloria learned as she fostered love in her partnership with William, was that 1) it is really fun to make her partner feel loved in the way he appreciated, and 2) William began to give her delightful, thoughtful surprise gifts in reciprocation.

It didn't take long, and the couple began to enjoy a rhythm of mutual nurturing and support, and Gloria's stress decreased significantly. Sure, kids and work and family always come with stressors, but with William's love and support she felt she could get through it with more calm and togetherness.

YOUR TURN

Identify your love language and the love languages of those close to you.

- ☐ My main love language is _____.

- ☐ Some examples of things that make me feel really loved and appreciated are _____. (Share with your partner!)

- ☐ My partner's main love language is _____.

- ☐ Some examples of things that make them feel really loved and appreciated are _____.

- ☐ My in-laws' love languages are _____.

- ☐ My parents' love languages are _____.

- ☐ My kids' love languages (right now*) are: _____.

- ☐ Others to think of are siblings, close friends, boss, colleagues, employees, helper friends, and kids' teachers.

Note: With impressionable young minds, your best bet is to know how they currently seem to feel love most, but expose them to all love languages so they can find out which they resonate with best as they get older.

Ego: Leave It at the Door

Oh, Ego, the S.O.B. that loves to wreak havoc. Ego is a sniper assassin of effective communication, finding its target at the most vulnerable time and pulling the trigger to make a small disagreement turn into a full-out battlefield. In order to have more productive communication within your relationships, *never* let your ego lead the way. Even if you *know* you're right, sometimes (ahem—most of the time) it's better to be supportive and listen than to be right. And yes, this is easier said than done!

One time Kyle was upset with me because I hadn't shared some plans I'd created for the day. He was angry not so much because I'd forgotten to tell him about it, but because I had a pattern of doing this. That frustration had built up to a breaking point for him. You see, I love having experiences. I like filling the calendar with all kinds of activities and events to look forward to. If you haven't been able to tell yet, I'm a total Debbie Doer. I also have such busy days that sometimes I forget who I told what to, including Kyle. I know you can relate or you wouldn't have picked up this book. My people!

Kyle shared—and to his credit, calmly—that he felt I wasn't keeping him in the loop enough. The fiery voice—my ego—inside my head immediately said, "WTF? *He's* getting mad at *me* for making plans, when he does the same sh*t to me?" (My ego has a bit of a potty mouth.) But then I told my ego to shut up, because I realized this was not my moment to create a world war.

Instead of retaliating, I realized it was Kyle's time to share what was in his heart. So I went into active listening mode, and chose not to make it about me and my ego and presumed positive intent. I heard him out. Then I said, "You're right." Because he was. Even if he sometimes did the same thing, it still wasn't right that I did it. And when I said, "I'll work on it," I meant it. I'm not perfect at it now, but I'm better than I was yesterday, and better than I was last month and a year ago.

What could've been hours of exhausting tears and yelling with possibly no good resolution turned into a five-minute conversation where I took responsibility for myself with compassion, ending in a hug and kiss and moving on.

See how calm that was? You are left with so much more space when you handle confrontations and relationship mishaps in this mindset. You're not only helping your partner by listening without your ego, but you're also helping yourself. Who needs to live in a space of anger and resentment? It's even more draining than your kid calling, "Mommy. Mommy. Mommy. Mommy" for an hour after they go to bed.

Now, because of how I handle things when he's upset, and because I've created enough goodwill with him, he'll leave his ego behind as well. That's not to say we never argue or bicker. But we've avoided most big, dramatic confrontational fights for over ten years. No outbursts of yelling, "*You* do this," "Well *you* do that!"

Putting your ego aside is essential to a productive resolution to any confrontation. If you've done something wrong, ego can prevent you from apologizing to make it right. Apologizing and taking accountability builds soooo much trust and goodwill and promotes all the good feels. When you genuinely apologize, you give permission for others to do the same—you model how to foster good communication, accountability, and maturity. And with kids, they see that adults aren't perfect—we make mistakes, and that's okay as long as we own them. They'll model this behavior as well because it will become the norm in your home.

As a leader or colleague, when you hold yourself accountable and admit your mistakes you foster a culture of accountability and thoughtfulness and allow others to do the same. It's a beautiful cycle of mutual respect when everyone can own up to their sh*t and lean on each other for support in an open and transparent way. So kick ego to the curb to enjoy more calm in relationship resolution!

Leaving your ego behind is a lot easier said than done. After all, ego is tied to our core and has a megaphone. Some ways that you can prevent ego from taking the wheel include practicing understanding, compassion, respect, and trust.

Understanding

Seeking understanding is the first step of being able to keep ego at bay and can be achieved with active listening. By putting yourself in a place of curiosity instead of defensiveness, you're able to get a clearer view of why the person you're talking to feels the way they do. So in my example with Kyle, I could say, "I understand you didn't feel heard when you asked if I would check in with you before making plans Saturday night."

Compassion

This can be reached by not only understanding but also feeling the feels of the other person. Imagine being in their position and feeling the discomfort they're in. I'm not saying you have to agree, but you can at least try to empathize with their position. In my example with Kyle, I could say, "I totally get that you feel like I didn't hear you when I made plans for Saturday night without checking in. Not being heard is a terrible feeling."

Respect

You know the golden rule—treat others the way you want to be treated. Always remember this rule whenever you are faced with a conflict.

Respect should be mutual in your partnership or relationship—if it isn't, there are bigger relationship concepts and topics you might want to look into that aren't written about in this book.

When you remember that you love and respect your loved one and don't want them to feel upset, you're more able to leave ego out of the conversation. Be patient, and you'll have your chance to share your feelings. But in the moment they're sharing, it's their turn. Let them speak their truth, without interrupting or invalidating their feelings, the same way you'd want to be heard when, inevitably, it will be your turn to share your own disappointment or upset. Try to avoid defensive or gaslighting statements like, "That's not true!" or "How could you think that I would do something like that?" These kinds of statements are disrespectful and don't promote a safe space for your partner to open up. They also sabotage any chance you have of being heard respectfully when it's your turn to speak. Instead, try saying something like, "I respect you and your feelings. Thank you for sharing and I am going to make a conscious effort to check in before making plans. Your time and ideas are important, and you may have had a different idea for how you wanted to spend the night."

Trust

The final step to effectively leave ego at the door is to practice trust. Remember, the other person is probably not intentionally trying to be hurtful and malicious. Remind yourself no human is perfect. Practice presuming positive intent. We never truly know what's happening for another human being. There are so many factors that lead to any one person's behaviors and decisions. When we trust that their heart is in a good place and that they are doing their best in the condition they're in, then ego won't get enough oxygen and will suffocate.

Further Connecting with Your Partner

We've covered a lot on how to connect with your community, colleagues, and friends already, but we need to talk a little bit more about close communication with your (if you have one) life partner. I think most people would agree when I say that the most important person to nail positive communication with is your partner, the one you chose to do all the life things with.

The goal of good communication with your partner is to foster love, respect, and appreciation. There's no other relationship like this. Partnership has its own section here because of the nuances of this dynamic and ever-evolving relationship—deep emotional agreements, life scheduling, finances, making and raising children, responding to and processing kid triggers, making big life decisions, careers, living environments, and so much more. Following I share various topics and modalities for creating a deep, authentic, and reciprocal life partnership through communication, all of which will have a huge impact on your calm.

Dreams and Ambitions

Every year starting on my birthday and leading up to the New Year (pretty much the whole month of December), Kyle and I talk about and make a plan for our dreams and ambitions for the upcoming year. This is another proactive versus reactionary approach to creating a successful, supportive relationship (leading to a calmer, less chaotic life). We talk about our intentions and the milestones we'd like to achieve for our family, as a couple, and as individuals for the year.

This practice doesn't have to be yearly, but it's easy to remember to do it when you attach it to an anniversary or a birthday or other regular event. Throughout the year you may think of something you want to pursue or a habit you want to create. Some ambitions will have goal dates and some will be evergreen. For example, in December of last year, I wanted to start being more hydrated to help with my energy. I didn't wait until my birthday to bring this up with Kyle, as I wanted to start right away. So I shared it with him as soon as I made the decision to drink a gallon of water a day, so that he could support me with my goal. Even if your partner isn't the one doing the activity with you, you need to let them in on your journey so they can understand and support you better. No mind-reading necessary!

So often, we have dreams and wish lists of what we'd like to do and accomplish, but it never leaves our own brains. Then we get resentful when the world doesn't line up for us to make it happen. Well, that sh*t's on us. We have to tell the world what we desire, not only to manifest it for ourselves but also to get the support we might need to follow through. As soon as Kyle knew I was trying to hydrate, he started offering me more cups of water when he was in the kitchen, asking me how my goal was going, and reminding me in the afternoon to drink up. He even surprised me with a new Hydro Flask. Had I not told him, I definitely would have had a harder time meeting my goal of drinking a gallon of water a day. By sharing your desires and goals with your partner, they will know you better. And through knowing comes understanding and more calm.

If you are so overwhelmed you don't even remember what the heck you want in life, I've included a handy questionnaire later in this chapter to help.

Calendar

Because having a calendar is so important, I am talking about it again. Creating a joint calendar helps everyone keep their sh*t together. There's no confusion about when events are happening when everyone keeps the calendar up-to-date. When is back-to-school night? Check the calendar. When is our double date planned? Check the calendar. When is your dentist appointment? Say it with me: Check the calendar.

Besides the obvious calendar items like important school and work events, put sex on the calendar. Yes, I am 100 percent serious here! Plan it. The anticipation of the date coming makes the romance even stronger. Plus, you can be sure to prepare, maybe by showering and putting on a little something sensual or seductive. This doesn't mean you're obligated. You obviously can decline when the time arrives. And you certainly can indulge spontaneously whenever you want, too. But isn't this a much simpler way to handle the "When are we having sex?" conversation? This is especially important when you have young kids and small privacy windows. AND you can reference back to the last time you had nooky. No more, "It's been a month!" Nope, honey, it's been three days. Check the calendar.

Our joint calendar has my "flow" week in it as well. That is definitely something Kyle appreciates knowing about. (Mama needs space, kiddos ... for the next couple of days—PMS is on the loose!)

Add anything and everything that can help your partner understand you better, know you better, beyond just the to-dos. EVERYTHING goes on the calendar.

Pro Tip: In most online calendars, you can create a custom calendar for you and your partner, so what they add to it shows up on your personal calendar and vice versa. You can code it with colors. How about red for your sexy calendar = red-hot?! And then toggle that calendar on or off so you can just see your work or home or partner's calendar.

Because I am a calendar nut, I have four calendars. I have calendars for work, family, sex + flow, and personal. Kyle has access to them all, and he can toggle between them to see what's important to him in the moment.

When you add an item to the calendar, tag everyone who is meant to be a part of that event. If you add to the joint calendar, everyone will see it, but it may not be clear who is responsible for taking the lead on that event. It's important for everyone to know who is responsible for any said event, so add your partner so it will show up on their personal/work calendar, if appropriate. Also, as discussed in Efficiency, don't forget to add items such as commuting to an appointment, grocery shopping, or catching up over Zoom with out-of-town family.

Before going gung-ho on the calendar and adding your partner to everything, it is important to talk about it all first. Before your next "family ops" meeting (explained below), make a running list of all of the topics and items you want to discuss and the responsibilities you want to share (your partner can do the same). In the meeting, you both can share everything going on for the week(s) ahead and discuss who will do what. I also use that meeting to share things newly scheduled, even if they aren't happening for a while, and remind Kyle of events that were scheduled a long time ago and are coming up soon.

Family Ops Meetings

I tell my clients to huddle up with their partner at least weekly when they start this new routine. Kyle and I do this as well, and we call it "family ops." Just like it works in the business world to keep your work team on the same page, this is a great technique to review what each of you has going on in the coming week and ask what you can do to support each other through it. I even bring an agenda to the meeting to make sure everything gets covered.

When you share goals with each other and get agreement from your partner on what specific support you'll receive from them (and vice versa), things will run more smoothly. A lot of stress is caused by lack of preparation, which forces you to react to (what feels like) last-minute requests, such as, "Hey I'm going for a run." Perhaps you'd just been with the kids all day counting down to when your partner gets home so you could go to the gym (or whatever your "you" thing is). And if there isn't a proactive agreement, the more that happens, the more resentment builds. So, when you're discussing your goals with your partner, get specific. Nail down the days and times you'll be working on your goal and they'll be working on theirs. That way, there will be no surprises and resentments. And if you're not feeling up to working on your goal during the agreed-upon time, don't get snotty if another time doesn't work for the other person. If you skip your allotted time for whatever reason, it's not your partner's duty to give up their (agreed-upon) need so you can fit in your missed time. Would it be a nice gesture and you'd totally want to have sex with them if they did? Sure. But they don't owe it to you.

I know this is sounding a lot like a business, but isn't running a family very similar? I've learned from years of applying my human resources background to my family how to manage time more efficiently so partners can make room for what they both need ahead of time rather than fighting for it in the moment.

You can include the kids in your meetings and discussions here, too! To know what's important to them and what they're working on will only help them succeed that much more. But remember, your kids' wishes and dreams are not all your responsibility to fulfill for them. You're a support for sure, but you shouldn't just add all of their stuff onto yours. Perhaps with smaller kids you can split up managing their goals with your partner as well, based on skill and desire level. It helps to know what your kids are really wishing for so you know what buttons to push to motivate them and what buttons you might be able to press to keep them calm.

At the simplest level, perhaps your kid is super into superheros. Next time they're wigging out over a hard worksheet from school, you can remind them that to be like Spider-Man (their dream), they could handle it a certain way. And you can certainly use their dreams as leverage for behavior that gives you space to breathe.

Roles and Responsibilities

I know what you're thinking. *Fine, Jenna, I'll put to-dos and my period, and fine, even sex into the calendar. But how do we come up with who is doing what and when? I don't want to start from scratch each week.*

If you don't have a clear division of ongoing roles and responsibilities at home, now is the time to clarify who does each ongoing task—like making meals, mowing the lawn, doing household improvements, folding laundry, washing dishes, watering plants, cleaning, paying bills, doing kid pick-ups and drop-offs? Feeling an imbalance of roles and responsibilities is one of the most prevalent topics with my coaching clients. Women typically feel they carry more (and not just more, *way* more) of the load of home responsibilities than their partner does. By discussing and agreeing on the division of your home's shared responsibilities, you'll have clarity and understanding of who does what and when, and can hold each other accountable.

You know that resentment you feel when you've been on your feet all day doing everything for everyone, and you arrive home to see the same heap of unfolded laundry sitting there in front of everyone, and no one even considers folding it? Because of course they all assume that you're going to do it—because you typically always do and they don't even think to "help." Right? WRONG. Setting up a clear "who does what" roles and responsibilities strategy will help avoid resentment of one person doing too many things and it will open lines of communication when the chaos of running a family gets confusing.

The best way to start your roles and responsibilities conversation is by telling your partner what you're up to with this whole *Chaos to Calm* thing. Then schedule some time to sit down together, with as few distractions as possible. Make a list of all the home responsibilities. Talk to your partner about how you'd love to share the list between you. Invite their feedback. Make the conversation as collaborative as possible. It doesn't have to be 50/50 but rather a distribution that (with ego out of the picture) feels fair to you both.

Here is a handy checklist to get you in the right state of mind prior to your discussion. If your partner can come to the meeting having read this as well, even better!

1. **Remember, you are first and foremost a TEAM! There is no "I" in *partnership*.** Okay, there is, but you see my point. Partnership is a team effort.

2. **Bring a list of everything you handle to your meeting.** This list is extremely satisfying to write. I guarantee you'll feel like a badass when you see this list. Your calendar items can help inform this list. Your partner should also make their own list of things they handle to bring to your discussion.

3. **At your meeting, combine your lists, and estimate the amount of time each task or responsibility takes.**

4. **Factor in the emotional importance of that role or responsibility to that person.** For example, if your partner was never picked up from school as a child and really wants to be that parent, they should be. Also, when choosing roles and responsibilities, factor in what each of your strengths and weaknesses are. Kyle hates making doctor and dentist appointments, and I love crossing calls like that off my list of things to do, so I make those appointments for our family. Win-win!

5. **You should not only review who does what, but also *when* (so you can agree on a reasonable time frame) and *how* (so you can discuss different methods).** For example, if everyone knows that laundry gets folded at night, then I won't need to be mad if there's a load waiting to be folded before dinner. Strategize tasks to have the most impact. Perhaps laundry day should be on Saturdays so everyone knows their full wardrobe on Sunday to plan for the week.

And finally, the most important step:

6. **What isn't on *your* list—LET. THE. F. GO.** Seriously, I mean it. Trust that your partner has their sh*t together. If they don't, trust they'll reach out if they need help. (If they don't, that's on them, not you; do not take on any guilty responsibility.)

You can always call another meeting to adjust the list at any time depending on work schedules, other life changes, or changing desires, but you have to stop thinking about what's on your partner's list and trust they will get it done in the manner they promised. If they don't, you can gently remind them, but presume positive intent before getting pissed off that the plants haven't been watered and lunches haven't been made yet. If your partner doesn't do their task to your liking, you need to let it go. Maybe your sock-folding skills are better, or you cut sandwiches cuter, but does it actually matter? If a task is really meaningful to you, then it's best to revisit the responsibilities conversation to make a trade.

YOUR TURN

Roles and Responsibilities

- [ ] Create a Roles and Responsibilities Chart for your family using the link in Resources on page 252. Fill them out so everyone will know what they are responsible for and can be accountable. I like to call it the Getting Sh*t Done List. This list identifies what the core tasks are, who is responsible for it, when they will do it, how they will do it, and additional notes as needed.

- [ ] After you've completed your Roles and Responsibilities Chart, repeat this line to each other: "I promise to ask for support when needed. And I will share with you if I can't do my usual responsibility." Yeah, I know that sounds silly to say out loud. But there should be some sort of conclusion that acknowledges that you have each other's back.

Dreams and Ambitions

- [ ] Pick one or more of the following prompts and journal your answers to reveal your desires.

  - I want to master a healthy habit I'm working on, which is: _____. With my partner's support, I'll do this (where, when, frequency): _____.
  - In my career, I'd like to _____ in the next year/month/week. With my partner's support, I'll do this (where, when, frequency): _____.

- Personally, I'd like to _____ in the next year/month/week. With my partner's support, I'll do this (where, when, frequency) _____.

- As a parent, I'd like to _____ in the next year/month/week. With my partner's support, I'll do this (where, when, frequency): _____.

- As a family member or friend, I'd like to _____ in the next year/month/week. With my partner's support, I'll do this (where, when, frequency): _____.

- In a year, I'd like my life to look like this: _____.

- How I'll help support my partner with their dreams and ambitions: _____.

- How I'll help support my kids with their dreams and ambitions: _____.

- How I'll help support myself with my dreams and ambitions: _____.

Discussion Tips: If you're still feeling lost on where to start on your dreams and ambitions, sit down with your partner and free-write a list. Ask them to write them down for you and vice versa. Say, "Tell me all your desires (sure, wink, wink, those too!), and then let's prioritize, because right now we can only handle so much. Let's figure out the timeline, and we can revisit them after we we give them a try."

Getting Your Partner on Board

I fully realize not everyone has a partner who is more than willing to make changes in the current family dynamic or take on more tasks. Even just the request could set off an argument. "I don't have time for this!" For those mamas who are a bit stuck in an antiquated partner dynamic, I conferred with Kyle to share tips on how someone could approach her partner, to maximize success.

Reasons to Support Your Partner (a Special Note from Kyle)

First off, you can use these concepts to open the conversation in the correct mindset (feel free to photograph or screenshot this section for them to read prior!).

The word *partner* implies a *team*, right? Just like any team sport, if your partner isn't thriving, neither will the team thrive. When you committed to each other, *you* became *we*. This isn't to say you have to lose your individual identity. In fact, quite the opposite. By getting on the same page with roles and responsibilities, it opens the door for more individual time and exploration.

Chances are you're not exactly the same person you were when you first fell in love. The idea behind sharing dreams and ambitions is not to add more to-dos to your list, but to show that you're going to meet your partner where they are now and share their set of desires. In return, your partner will share theirs. Doesn't that sound awesome?

Tips for Getting Your Partner on Board

Approach the conversation with your partner in one of two ways:

1. **Areas where you need help—*from your partner*—to achieve your goals and feel fulfilled.**

2. **Areas where you need help—*from a hired source*—to achieve your goals and feel fulfilled.**

You can see that there really isn't an option for you to not get support of some kind, right?

Brainstorm the various ways the conversation can go. Then you'll be prepared for anything.

Create the ideal time and space for the conversation. Don't try to have this discussion when you're running late somewhere or when you know your partner is stressed. Use a "third space"—a concept that comes from the business world where the first space is your desk at work, the second space is a large meeting space designated for meetings, and a third space is a neutral, inspiring location that allows the person to not be in total work mode but to be influenced more by the surrounding and the person they're speaking with. This location doesn't have to be outside of the home; it could be the back patio. I just wouldn't have it in the bedroom or your home office.

Set the climate for your conversation. Bring your most positive, "Let's figure this out together" energy. Your energy will set the tone. If your energy is slumped, victimized, or defensive, your conversation won't be as fruitful. Come into the conversation with energy that is empowered, engaged, and open, and your partner will follow suit.

Look for your anchors first. What is working well and makes you both feel calm and energized? Point that out. Then invite your partner to share theirs.

Frame to your partner how you'd like them to participate in the conversation. Say something like, "I need you to just hear me" or "I love your ideas, but what I need right now is for you to hear me out." Or perhaps it's, "I need you to hear me and contribute your ideas" or "I need you to hear me and really help me and give me your guidance."

Talk about your pain points. Share your pain points and problem areas, and discuss the reason they're painful for you, and how it contributes to the happiness of the house.

Avoid conflict-inducing language. This is not a dictatorship; it is a partnership. Use words and phrases like "As a partnership, my needs are _____" and give your partner the same opportunity.

Make the conversation bigger than the both of you. A bigger vision for you as a couple and for your family will excite your partner about the future you want to create with them.

Use the word *we* more than *you*—remember, partner = team! For example, you might say, "I believe we could become a healthier family, and here's how." And if your partner doesn't have the same desire to do that, tell them you are burnt out and therefore unable to show up for them as a partner anymore.

Take responsibility for your part of it. What can you start to change in yourself?

Stay practical. Tell your partner what you need and how they can best show up for you in a practical sense, or your partner (especially a man) will go into their cave.

Point out what's going well with your partner's support. If you're trying to get support from your partner but your words make them feel insufficient, it won't be productive.

Speak with confidence. Don't assume a victim mentality.

Own your responsibility. Don't expect your partner to solve all your problems. When you put an immense responsibility on someone else to make your life better, you'll never be satisfied.

Stay calm. Calm is a frequency, and you want to match the frequency/vibration/harmony in your presence in the conversation. Don't come at your partner in a stressed or intense vibration/energy. Instead, set the tone and model calm and open-mindedness.

Take one thing at a time. Don't present too many changes at once. Take things in bite-size pieces, the items you need to tend to urgently, so your partner isn't thinking everything will be different and panic.

Start with one meeting, knowing there will be more. Don't try to create the entire plan and conversation in one sitting. Ease them into the discussion by having the dreams and ambitions conversation a few times in smaller increments.

Touch base with your partner as you work on your goals. They might be able to help!

Touch base on your progress regularly. Annually, at minimum. Time it with your anniversary!

Potential Reactions Your Partner May Have and How to Deal with Them

If this is a new conversation, your partner may feel they are being criticized or you're accusing them of not doing enough. Men can feel threatened—they may think, "I am giving all I have to you and this family, how can I give more?" Men, generally speaking, don't want to mess up. When men hear something is wrong, they're wired to take failure very seriously and they can either get defensive or shut down, at least initially. Make sure you are respecting your partner's mindset as well as your own:

Man/Partner: *I'm overwhelmed but projecting I'm fine.*

Woman/Other Partner: *I'm just expected to do all the things, manage them well, and be okay with it. And I'm NOT.*

Shared: *We are both struggling in our own ways. We do have choices, even if it feels like we don't at times. So let's help each other get to the future we're striving for together.*

Think about how the conversation could go. Do any of these examples sound familiar? Here are some possible replies:

"But that's not how things usually are. Why do things have to change?"
"Because if we both continue down this path, we're both going to suffer. We need to find a better way."

"But I am too busy/have no time. How would I fit in what you're asking me to do?"
"Let's both look at our calendars/agendas and reassess what our priorities are and take it from there."

"I do all of these things already! This is coming from a place of overwhelm on your side."
"I appreciate everything you do, and it may feel like I'm asking for a lot right now, but I really need your support to help me figure this out, because I'm drowning."

"Why is your thing more important than my thing?"
"My greatest desire is that we *both* can figure out together how we get to do what's important to us so we can be as happy and as present to the family and each other as possible."

"What about me? I need time for me, too."
"I want to support you *and* I want you to support me in everything I do, so let's figure this out together."

"I'm not good at these things."
"We've been able to figure out so many 'first times' together, and we'll figure this one out, too. And, I think you'd be great at this!"

Communication Tips for Every Level

Beginners. If you're a beginner at having any form of these types of conversations with your partner, you can't jump into a world peace–size conversation right off the bat. You have to start small (and I know it's hard to wait for more calm), but you are trying not to add more stress to your life (with partner conflict), so you have to take it one conversation at a time.

There's never a "perfect time" to approach sensitive topics, so you have to make the time. Don't say, "Honey, we need to talk" in a vague way, but say, "When is a good time for you to talk about something important to both of us?" You aren't trying to push them into something; you are trying to make it collaborative. "I'm noticing we're both pretty overwhelmed and we're not getting to do all the things we used to do or want to do. I'd love to talk about how we can rethink our day-to-day routines and to help each other manage everything we need but also get what we need so we can show up the best we can and not lose ourselves and our relationship in the chaos." Or simply try saying, "I miss you, I miss me, I miss us. Can we make some time to figure out how to make more time for us?"

Intermediates. If you have decent baseline communication between the two of you already, but there is a shift in the dynamic that has changed things (having kids, changing jobs) and there are now gaps in the way things are going, then you can jump right to the point. You might say, "Wow, I'm experiencing a lot of overwhelm and I would love to have your partnership and support so we can catch these moments of stress now, as early as possible, and figure out how to overcome them together and get back on track." Then you can go right into scheduling a time to have a longer discussion.

Advanced. You are adept at communicating hard issues, but maybe your relationship has gotten a little too comfortable/lazy in the chaos and you need a quick intervention. You may have a code word set up for putting yourself in time-out or to express the need for time with your partner. You can skip the setup and go right to your code word: "Babysitter?" Or that look your partner knows. "Things are getting more overwhelming—something has shifted in the force—and I think we need to look over our structure right now." You have a go-to place for these talks. For Jenna and I, it's "Cocktail at Stillwater?" or "Meet me on the balcony at 7?"

When All Else Fails

If you find yourself doing everything and are made to feel guilty for wanting to do anything for yourself, or you're made to feel like your request or needs are a burden to your partner, you may need to reevaluate your relationship. If you're unable to approach your partner with your exhaustion and overwhelm, if they don't show signs of wanting to support you, if you feel guilty for asking and are unable to get a good self-care practice in, or if your partner can't even be open to the conversation, that is *not* a healthy relationship and you should seriously consider your future with that person, starting with couples therapy. That type of relationship died with the dinosaurs! Here are some words you can use in this case: "This is not working for me. This needs to change. This way of living is not sustainable for me." Look far into your life and figure out what will eventually drive you insane or keep you sane. And move toward sanity.

A true partner, even if they're equally overwhelmed, will make the time to get it right with you. It may take time to make adjustments that work, and you may need to tweak things over time. It won't happen overnight. But a true partner will work with you on this. Your partner should want to build a regular and consistent check-in with you. If you have extreme stress in life, you should check in every day; if you are in a longer season of overwhelm, check in weekly. Never let it go longer than a week. Err on daily practice.

Communicating with Kids

Just as effective communication with your partner is incredibly important, so is communication with everyone else who lives in your household. Your home should be a sanctuary to all who live inside.

The challenge is that kids know exactly what to say and do to make you want to burn your sanctuary to the ground. Communicating with kids is even more challenging than with your partner because it is ever-evolving as they grow. Your children's brains are changing constantly, and the way that you approach communication with them needs to evolve as they do. Yes, what worked for you last week may not work this week. Yes, you thought you had this parent thing down and then a developmental milestone hit and all of the progress you made disappears into the abyss. Having been in the education field for more than fifteen years and currently raising kids aging between preschool to teenagerdom, I see both at home and in the educational setting that kids tend to tune us out.

Why Kids Tune You Out Sometimes

Most of our communication with children is pretty one-way. It's estimated that kids get told a direction or what to do approximately once per minute (see Resources on page 252).

"Put on your shoes."
"Sit still."
"Wash your hands before dinner."
"Do your homework."

They even get told who and when to hug people: *"Give grandma a hug!"*

Somehow we've gone from a society of kids barely being supervised to parents hovering over their kids' every move. Think about it, the majority of a kid's day is getting told what to do, whether at home, at school, or in after-school activities. So when given the opportunity to be part of a discussion and share ideas and thoughts, they relish it. Children love being involved in family discussions and plans. It's surprising how much they can offer and what they can do when we let them.

To create more calm in your home, get your kids on board and involved with plans and chores. Have the dreams and ambitions and roles and responsibilities discussion with them, too.

Kyle and I sat down with our kids when they were ten, nine, and seven, and shared that there are a lot of home responsibilities and tasks, and that we were overwhelmed with all there was to do. We shared openly about the amount of time it took to do all the home things, like setting the table while making dinner and then clearing the table, cleaning up after, doing the dishes, and loading the dishwasher. We let them know how it was hard for us to get other things done that brought us happiness, like playing games with them and just being together, when there were always chores to be done and cleaning up to do. We asked them for suggestions on how we could make it easier for us and how we could all work together as a team to support each other and our household. It was at that moment that they suggested they help around the house and that we create a chore wheel. We brainstormed chores that could be on the wheel, and ultimately they made the final list and the wheel and decided on the cadence of it being turned every week.

Family dinners are a great time to connect and find out what's important to your kids. No matter how busy your family is, it is so important to have at least one touch point a day where everyone comes together. For us, that's being together over dinner. It's in these moments that you have an opportunity to connect with each other and not just direct everyone where they need to go and what they need to do.

During dinner we have a ritual of sharing our highs and lows of the day, called "rose, bud, and thorn." We share a favorite part of the day (rose), something we are looking forward to (bud), and something that didn't go so well (thorn). Then, we share something we are grateful for that day. Night after night, as everyone hears each other's sharings, we better understand and build empathy toward each other. I find it interesting what the kids remember of each other's sharings and themes across weeks. You may even start to notice less resistance and conflict. They'll feel more like the family is a team.

Parents Are Not Robots

I don't want my kids to think I'm an impermeable robot. I show my kids vulnerability and accountability. I don't hide my emotions from them, most of the time. In building and maintaining a positive relationship with our kids, we need to show them we're human and not hide the parts of ourselves we don't like, are afraid of, or think we don't want our kids to see. Sh*t gets to me. I have thresholds, and I break down when they're crossed. I don't hide that from the kids. I own it and set the example that we are all perfectly imperfect humans. What really matters is that they take accountability and do their best.

When the kids were younger and as they continue to evolve, we helped them communicate how they're feeling by giving names for moods. I love really hard, but like everyone ever in the history of humanity, I have ups and downs in energy and capacity. And sharing that with the kids is an important part of us having effective communication and calm with each other.

When any of us is feeling emotional and we don't have a conscious reason for it, we call it being "banana." When I notice one of them in a funk and they don't have an answer for me when I ask them what's going on, I will ask, "Are you feeling banana?" If the answer is yes, we all know that means to give that person space and they will come back to us when they are feeling more grounded and ready to interact. We all under-stand that feeling "banana" means that someone is having an emotional moment, not necessarily brought on by any one person or event, and that they just need to process their emotions and move through banana on their own. Being that I have more self-awareness, when I am feeling banana, it's typically around my flow and I share that with them also. It's okay if your kids know that hormones exist. I'll say, "I have a lot of feelings right now and so I might have less patience than I usually do." Having heard this almost every month for their entire lives, they know not to take it personally if I get snappy. It's just my own form of being banana. That way, they know I'll need extra space that day, and it's in a lighthearted way they know has nothing to do with them. They in turn do the same thing when they feel that way. This way, we all empathize with each other.

Handling Interruptions

You know how kids have that radar where as soon as you sit down to do some work or read or anything for yourself, they immediately sense it and that's the time they desperately need you for *all the things*?

Before you drop what you're doing and create chaos in your body (that sick feeling when you're doing one thing but really need to be doing something else), do not feel guilty! You do not have to drop what you're doing to watch them attempt a somersault badly for the twentieth time or restart their movie for them or play tea. The more often you do that, the more your kids will get in the habit that you're at their beck and call, and that is not their fault. I mean, sure, if the kid is holding your prescrip-tion of Ambien and shaking it like a maraca, drop everything.

Here is what you can say when your child wants to play and you're busy: "Oh Alex, I *love* that you want to play Candyland with me! I'm in the middle of finishing this report for work, but I can't wait to play with you at 5 p.m.!" Will Alex throw down a tantrum or continue whining? Maybe.

But by not giving in and setting expectations, you both get what you want and need: work time and play together time. You're not only doing yourself a service by setting these boundaries, but you're also setting a great example for Alex of a healthy way to manage multiple demands at the same time.

Also, did you know that you don't have to play f'ing Candyland if you don't want to? Offer a different game instead. As parents, we somehow feel like we have to do and enjoy everything our kids are interested in. And sure, we can do some of that. It keeps us close to our kids to know what Pokemon card they're searching for and care about it along with them. But you don't have to sit on the floor and hurt your back and move your token through the candy cane forest mindlessly if you don't want to. What your kid really wants is some quality time with you. If you say that you'd love to play but prefer a different game, your child will most likely not protest.

As children typically do, they also always want our attention when we are engaged with someone else. If a child wants to get your attention but you are already in another conversation, have them touch your hand or arm. Tell them that you are listening or talking to someone else and that you want to hear what they have to say. "The best way for me to know that you want to tell me something is to put your hand on my arm or my hand." Then she knows that you need her, and won't be saying, "Mom, Mom, Mom." This way I am not upset or distracted and the person I am already talking to doesn't get upset or feel like you're not paying attention to them. I explain, "I want to give you all of my attention and hear what you have to say and I can't do that while I am talking/listening to someone else. When I am finished here, I will be with you and hear everything you want to tell me."

Chores and Rewards

As parents, it's our job to set kids up to be prepared for life outside of home. These growing pains can be uncomfortable, and when you institute a chore wheel or a system for getting more help from them, you may get a bit of pushback at first. You may have to accept a job done around the house inferior to how you'd do it. But worse would be doing everything for our kids and they end up leaving home not knowing how to pack a lunch or wash their clothes. When you sit down with your kids to talk about chore distribution, tell them as a family you want to get their input. Tell them why the meeting is happening, and that as a team the duties of the home need to be shared. Share the why, get their input and ideas from the get-go, and they'll be so much more invested. Kids have an innate desire to be helpers and when communicated in that way, they are more willing to pitch in.

My kids started packing their own lunches at around nine to twelve years old. I make sure to have appropriate ingredients on hand, and they know the varying components of what they need to pack for themselves. Primarily, they know to pack a main meal that includes protein, fruit, veggies, and a carby snack. I supervised this for a few weeks and now they do it entirely on their own and I use that time to literally do anything besides make lunches. Starting from when they could reach the table, we also had our kids set the table and clear it before and after dinner.

Once the chores have been allocated, it's important to keep a team mentality and pitch in when needed. For example, when it was my daughter Miya's job to empty the dishwasher, but she had a heavy homework night one evening, I asked my son Skye to step in. I was busy getting ready to go out (yes, you'll go out again too, I promise!). When I asked Skye to step in, I didn't bark an order. I said, "Skye, Miya is neck-deep with a homework assignment, Sage is too little to reach the dishes, and I'm not done getting ready. Can you help pitch in to the team by emptying the dishwasher?" Kids will be more apt to pitch in when they know how valued their contribution is. And they also know that at some point when they need extra help, the rest of the team will step in and have their back.

I've found that kids are generally willing to help. Given some context and letting them know why it's so important and helpful to you, they will generally be happy to pitch in and be seen as a "helper." I know that some parents don't believe that asking kids to help around the house is important or necessary—and maybe it's not part of your home culture right now. But I believe it helps make a more unified, helpful culture when there is an underlying sense of teamwork. It could be as simple as, "Can you help me by holding this door open so I can get rid of the garbage?" Kids as young as two can do that!

Having a list of standard chores divided up will help you make these decisions instinctually. If the kids push back, I pull out the, "We are all in this together, and I am very busy making dinner. I noticed you've already finished your homework and aren't doing anything right now, so it would be super helpful to me and I would really appreciate it if you could do this one thing. Thank you so much!" If I need them to fold their laundry and put it away, I'll point out that I did my part of the teamwork, having sorted, washed, and dried it, and now it's up to them.

YOUR TURN

Four chores I can assign my kids are:

- ☐ Who and when:
- ☐ Who and when:

- ☐ Who and when:
- ☐ Who and when:

Ideas to consider:

- ☐ Make bed
- ☐ Match socks
- ☐ Take clothes to the laundry room
- ☐ Move laundry from washer to dryer
- ☐ Feed pets
- ☐ Set the table, clear the table
- ☐ Help cook and prepare meals
- ☐ Make own and others' lunches

- ☐ Put groceries away
- ☐ Get the mail
- ☐ Load dishwasher, empty dishwasher
- ☐ Fold and put away laundry
- ☐ Take out trash
- ☐ Vacuum
- ☐ Sweep
- ☐ Walk pet
- ☐ Clean the bathroom

Interruption plan

- ☐ When my kids interrupt me mid-task, I'll say _____ instead of dropping what I'm doing.

OWN YOUR CALM: COMMUNICATION RECAP

Communicating well with those closest to you increases calm and nurtures healthier relationships by lessening misunderstandings, creating visibility, and assigning ownership on who does what, ensuring everyone is on the same page. Effective communication strategies to get the support you need include:

- ✓ Active listening
- ✓ Being proactive
- ✓ Assuming positive intent
- ✓ Love language mastery
- ✓ Leaving ego at the door
- ✓ Sharing dreams and ambitions
- ✓ Utilizing a shared calendar
- ✓ Getting clear about roles and responsibilities
- ✓ Connecting authentically with children and sharing household responsibilities

care

How to Take Care of the Most
Important Person in Your Life: You

> "I have come to believe that caring
> for myself is not self-indulgent.
> Caring for myself is an act of survival."
>
> —AUDRE LORDE

WE'VE ALL HEARD ABOUT THE importance of self-care. In fact, self-care is *so important* that the whole purpose of this book is to help you streamline your life so you can fit more of it in. While those around you may benefit from you taking care of yourself, your self-care is not for anybody else—it is for *you*.

We all have activities, practices, and rituals that restore us. Think about the things you do that make your spirit happy, that make you feel connected to your deeper self, that evaporate stress and bring calm. These are not meant to be things you do to better yourself, although many can, but things you do that enable you to *be* your best and happiest self. Self-care is when you, at your core, feel nurtured and cared for.

Making You a Priority

Self-care is not a new concept—go online or watch TV and there are ads galore promoting "self-care" with this or that product or service. "Get these bath bombs and candles for your self-care," "Your face routine is your self-care," "This miracle serum is an integral part of self-care." Blah blah blah—noise, stuff, marketing . . . While these ideas sound nice—who wouldn't want to lie in a quiet room while someone dotes on you?—it's not a practical, affordable, or consistent solution for everyone.

Over the years, I've learned some tricks to unlock self-care time and how to use that time to my greatest benefit, and though these rituals might not resonate for everyone, I've found they go a long way in bringing out my best, healthiest self.

- Listening to an audiobook (I often do this while folding laundry or brushing my teeth—a meditative chore or task that doesn't take any brain cells to do and I feel doubly accomplished after I'm done).

- Heading out to a cafe to have tea and read my book once a week while Kyle or a sitter puts the kids to bed. Those two hours a week are effing precious to me.

- Going out for a run or hike and listening to my audiobook or music on Saturday mornings. Even if I can only run for ten minutes, connecting to nature and my body during that time changes my mood for the rest of the day.

- Applying a Trader Joe's $2 face mask before bed.

- Meditating for three minutes in the morning and the middle of the day.

- Stretching for five minutes before bed.

- Taking a bath.

Self-care doesn't mean you have to take a whole "Self-care Sunday" or spa day. I'm talking about integrating mini self-care practices and rituals into your daily routines and habits. Self-care doesn't have to be a huge undertaking that you spend hours planning and tons of money and effort on.

What I'm talking about in this chapter are little rituals, activities, or rest in between all the work you do for others, to care for yourself and treat yourself well. The goal of a solid self-care practice is to bring yourself to a state in which you can show up for yourself and everyone around you with more calm and groundedness. By taking care of your mind (your thinking and thoughts), body, and spirit, you will be able to show up as your best self and in turn be a better parent, role model, colleague, and partner. If you are not feeling depleted all the time and giving so much of yourself away without adding and giving input into your reserves, you are going to max out. I've been there so many times and I'm sure you have as well. You feel like there is nothing left to give. You feel helpless and defeated.

Clichéd advice like "Put your own oxygen mask on first" and "Fill up your own cup first" have good intentions and are valid. But they're not enough. They don't convey enough importance on caring for yourself. It is not a nice-to-have. It is not only in times of emergency. It is a daily necessity. But, if you're anything like me, some of this advice can feel like another "to-do" to plan and execute every day. And the last thing any busy parent needs is another task.

Rather than offer you more clichéd advice, I'm going to tell you about circles of support. As individuals and as a part of a community, we all have a responsibility to take care of ourselves before we can take care of others. To get on top of problems and seize opportunities, it takes everybody working together. If we want to own our calm and be able to contribute and support our community and society as a whole, we can do this by using circles.

In Richard Branson's autobiography, *Finding My Virginity*, he explains that he draws a circle around himself and makes sure that everything inside of that circle is working well. Is he taking care of his body with exercise and healthy eating? Is his work-life balance in check? Once he feels his "self" circle is taken care of and supported, he can widen the circle to include his family and friends. He then does everything in his power to help them and make sure that they are supported. When family and friends are in a good spot, he then widens the circle to incorporate neighbors and immediate community. If there are issues with them, he helps. After that, the circle widens to include society at large.

Imagine if everyone drew circles around themselves, and upon feeling secure, progressively widened their circles. All people would feel connected, loved, cared for, and a sense of belonging.

In this chapter, I'll show you how to support your innermost circle by integrating self-care into your daily life without it feeling like a burden or just another to-do.

Self-care is a key component of calm because if you are not taken care of at the deepest, most fundamental level, it is impossible for you to care for others in your calmest capacity. More than anyone else, your kids will benefit from a cared-for parent, rather than one who is barely scraping by. And yes, sometimes all we *can* do is scrape by, but it is possible to do more than that. With a little up-front energy (let's get proactive!), you can feel more grounded and nurtured through small self-care habits and routines that will greatly amplify you and your ability to show up as a partner and parent. You will be able to live in calm.

So who is going to create the space for you to practice self-care? Look in the mirror, my friend. *You* are the person who will make you the highest priority in your life. It must be and can only be you. No one can exercise for you. No adult is going to floss another grown-ass person's teeth for them. No one can choose what food you eat or hobbies you are passionate about.

Every person needs to look out for themselves first and foremost. And when you are cared for, you can show up for your family. And when your family is cared for, you can show up for your community. You are the most important person in your kids' lives. They need a healthy and cared-for parent—you can't show up for your kiddos if you are ill or injured. No one wins when you are suffering. Don't be a martyr. There is no messiah waiting to give you a medal and a mimosa for killing yourself to be present for everyone in your life while sacrificing your own needs.

When I moved to the San Francisco Bay Area with Kyle and the kids, I left my "village." I knew no one, was unfamiliar with the area, and became a full-time mom seemingly overnight. I felt out of place and isolated, especially after Sage was born, and it was like my body and soul weren't "me" anymore.

I wasn't happy and I had to figure myself out. I became a wife and mother and a San Franciscan all within about a month, and at the same time I needed to find a new job, and then shortly after that I was pregnant with Sage. I had no idea where I fit in the world anymore. It was like self-identity whiplash. I had to get reacquainted with me and reestablish who I was in this new season and phase of my life.

I felt shackled to my home. I told Kyle I felt like a prisoner in our own home, and that I needed a year to figure things out. He listened to what was in my heart, and I took that year to focus inward. To figure out what lit me up physically, psychologically, and spiritually.

I found the book *Pussy: A Reclamation*, by Regena Thomashauer, and it hit me at my core. I read this book and thought, "F yes! This is exactly what I need. I need to rediscover what makes me feel good." I needed to reconnect to my inner goddess, rediscover what I love about myself, and make decisions from a space of pleasure and connection to my body, from a place of joy and self-love.

I found that when I made decisions from this place, I was able to be clearer about what I wanted and needed to do. And things went incredibly smoothly at home when I approached my family from this place as well. Anything that came up—from what to wear, to what to make for dinner, to answering questions from the kids and Kyle—I approached from the place that brought me joy and pleasure, and it made answering those questions so much easier and my responses were better than I had ever given before. It's not that I was "me me me" all the time. Bringing my family joy and pleasure was high on the list too. But I had forgotten about myself along the way and I brought myself back, front and center. When you no longer struggle with your own happiness, your relationships are no longer a struggle either.

Start incorporating what brings you joy. They don't have to be big things! Maybe wearing a bright color brings you joy. For me, it was reviving big accessories (hello, hoops!) and meditation.

"Pay attention to the whispers, so you won't have to listen to the screams." This saying is a Cherokee proverb that promotes being proactive. When you respond to something when it's small, it's a lot easier to remedy before it turns into something huge. There's a similar concept in the business world, where small problems not attended to eventually lead to bigger business issues, especially as a business grows. Think about it: If there's a rodent living in the walls of your home, instead of waiting for it to die, you have to find the rodent's access point and close it off, or you might end up with rodent babies as roommates. Ew. You will be a lot calmer knowing that you were able to prevent more creatures from living in your walls than stressing when they have created a home of their own and invited their cousins to live with them. If your child is having a hard time on an assignment, rather than assume it's just an issue with one assignment, make sure it's not an issue with understanding a concept, something that could bleed into more assignments and their understanding of bigger concepts. If you don't master addition properly, you definitely won't be able to fathom multiplication.

Managing Energy

A big part of caring for your spirit is observing and nurturing your body's energy. We all have days we feel more energetic and "on," and days we feel like the character Sad from the movie *Inside Out*, slowly slugging through the day. As we talked about in the Efficiency chapter, for women, this is often surrounding our moon cycles.

During your cycle, make note of when you feel most energetic. Shade those days in green on your calendar, so you know to book your more intense work meetings or activities that week if you can. Then, as you enter your luteal phase and your body might feel in the middle—not super gung-ho but not dragging either—shade that time frame in yellow. Lastly, during your least energetic days, shade that time in pink so you know it's not a smart idea to book difficult appointments or take on new projects, and you can practice compassion for yourself during that time. I tell my kids that it feels like there is a storm in my brain on the days directly before and on the first day of my period. This way they know that if I'm not as patient or I'm crankier than usual, it's because there are hurricanes and tsunamis crashing everywhere in my mind and they will pass soon.

Pro Tip: You can download apps onto your phone that track your cycle and provide insights on energy as well as physical and mood changes. You can get daily notifications on what to expect that day based on where you are in your cycle.

Your energy could also ebb and flow based on the season or the weather. Colder weather may energize you or make you lethargic. When you feel your body resisting the demands you're giving it, listen. Learn. I know you can't always choose when you need to do what all the time, but in this new proactive land you're living in, you can do a lot to prevent burnout and fetal-position crying fits from overexhaustion.

You know those magical moments when you feel like you're on fire? When you're setting sh*t up and knocking it down. Your ideas are flowing! You even played a couple rounds of Sorry! with your kids without feeling like you wanted to poke your eyes out with those little phallic pieces. Ride that wave, mama! Capitalize on your momentum!

Being Social Takes Physical, Mental, and Spiritual Energy

Being social can be—for me—very invigorating. Spending time talking to interesting people, hanging out with friends, being engaged in an intellectual conversation—they are all energy givers. And there are times when being with people can be exhausting. I find myself so energized and excited when I am around people, but as soon as I am out of that context, I am drained and need a nap.

Just because socializing does not require physical exercise doesn't mean that your body may not be exhausted after being at a social event. After a big event for the kids' school or after Kyle's band plays, I have zero energy to be social because I have a social energy bucket and it only has so much capacity. Sometimes I am just not capable of hanging out and shooting the sh*t after an event; I need to put on my pjs and be horizontal. I am an introverted-extrovert, who needs time alone to recharge, but also gets a lot of energy being around people. If you are the kind of person who gets energy from being alone, be sure to give yourself plenty of alone time before going to a social event.

Understanding your needs is pivotal in being able to effectively care for yourself. Self-care is knowing what you need so you can make sure you get it. In the name of self-care, I invite you to take notice of your social energy levels and meet your needs accordingly.

When you understand your energy flows and cycles, you can be proactive in scheduling self-care and recharging time before and after energy-depleting activities.

I am not promising that life will be all sunshine and rainbows once you get self-care reined in. What I am saying is that you will be able to more easily adapt, make changes on the fly, and know how to support yourself when plans go awry, your flow gets derailed, or inevitable life things happen that thwart all of your best-laid plans.

Maybe you always go for a run after dinner as self-care. But that morning, your car broke down and you had to walk two miles to get to the mechanic. So you adjust to do something more mellow that evening. Or, if you can't do your self-care routine at all because you had to take a kid to urgent care, you can shift your self-care moment. Maybe if your partner is with you, you could go for a walk around the block or go to the waiting area and listen to a song or write in your journal. There are ways to nurture yourself even in the hardest of moments. It is possible to shift your self-care to match the circumstance and energy you're needing or feeling.

Self-Care Looks Different in Different Moments

There are ways to manage your self-care on a regular basis—rituals to help regulate your mind and body, like exercise. During times when your physical energy is lower, that's when you need to shift your self-care to quieter things, such as listening to music, doing a puzzle, taking a bath, watching a movie, going for a walk, meditating, or doing an art activity.

I have found that when my family goes through a health crisis or some other major event, I do much better when I shut down some of the more stimulating activities in my routine—as fun as they may be—so I can rest my heart and mind. I have also found that sometimes saying no to those meetups is saying yes to me when I need to preserve more of my energy for myself or my family. My emotional and physical energies are both very low when I am needed to give extra to my family, and I've become aware of that. To make sure I don't completely lose track of myself while caring for my family, I use what limited energy I have toward a short workout, because I know that exercising enables me to show up with a clearer mind and more patience.

TONIA
the touchy

A client told me that when she feels overwhelmed she can't be touched. It is just too much for her. Her kids will try to get her attention by tapping her or her husband will try to hold her while she is in the middle of making dinner, and that unwanted touch makes her blood boil and her skin crawl. This is a common response to overstimulation. I shared with her that when we are overloaded with stimulation, our sympathetic nervous systems are on high alert. Mothers have stimuli coming from all directions—albeit some of it can be "good" or "positive" stimulation, but it's stimulation nonetheless. Sometimes normal life things get too stimulating, like hearing your kids laughing, seeing people coming in and out of the kitchen, hearing doors slammed shut, smelling nail polish, hearing the blender, being touched by your partner or kids, and even thinking. Mothers endure so much auditory and visual stimulation that when we add the mental load of the running lists of to-dos and problem solving that is being held in our brains at all times, it's no wonder we get overwhelmed. On an "average" day, in an "average" household, in the late afternoon/early evening, there are 2.4 kids running around, and you are:

- thinking about what to make for dinner
- listening to the kids ask for snacks

- digesting the day in your head
- reminding the kids to bring you their lunch boxes so that you can clean and refill them
- listening to your partner tell you about their day
- thinking about all the things you have to take care of before you go to bed
- creating a running list of to-dos for tomorrow
- getting the kids ready for baths
- thinking about getting drinks and snacks for the school/sports team
- realizing you're out of milk

Right there—that is more than enough stimuli for any one person to endure. And that is an average parent on an average day. No wonder Tonia didn't want to be touched! Her sensory system was already overloaded. I shared with Tonia that not wanting to be touched was completely normal when she was feeling overwhelmed. Her sensory system was overloaded with data and it could not accept one more stimulus. I suggested Tonia talk with her family about physical boundaries and her stimulus overload. We also agreed that if she found herself overwhelmed and not sure why, she should go someplace quiet, with as little stimulation as possible, for even just a few minutes, so she could be away from the noise, regulate her nerves, and quiet her mind.

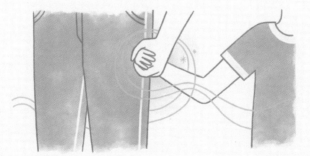

When you are overwhelmed, take a breath, calm your nervous system, and reenter when your body has had the opportunity to chill. It's okay to tell your partner and kids you need a moment and that you are going to take a breath outside, lie down on your bed for a quick nap, take a shower, or meditate for two minutes. This is your self-care. This is how you take care of your needs and prioritize your calm. After you reenter, you will be more available for answering the "Mom, Mom, Mom" questions and be more open to being touched.

If you have plans and are currently feeling overwhelmed or overstimulated, you have the right to cancel your plans in the name of self-care without guilt. This is the perfect time to practice being proactive and communicating effectively. If others are disappointed in you for not being there, that's their emotion to manage, not yours. All you can do is be as honest, open, and communicative as possible. When you choose a supportive community and are as proactive with your communication as you can be (by letting them know you're tired for whatever reason), they will understand. If not, defer to the family management skills you learned in the Community chapter to try to let go and not allow their unreasonable expectations to harm your spirit.

I have done this on multiple occasions. I was supposed to have a coffee date with a friend and told her I needed to cancel because I would not be good company that day. I was feeling quite overwhelmed and needed to spend the limited time I had while the kids were at school to just be alone. I cared about my friend dearly and knew that she had stuff going on also, but I was in no place to really hear her and show up as a good friend. She totally understood and told me that she would check in on me in a week or two. I was so grateful that she didn't put added pressure on me to tell her when I would be ready to meet up.

During that same time, a friend called and wanted to talk about a breakup she had just gone through. Knowing that my emotional bandwidth was entirely empty, I told her that I had only a few minutes to connect and had to keep our call short. For those few minutes, I was able to hold enough space to listen to her, but then I had to tell her I had to go. Even when a friend is "in need," you still have to hold your own boundaries. You are your most precious person to take care of and it's not your responsibility to be on-call for everyone in your life.

Self-care is not a one and done. Calm is not a one and done. Calm is a continuous, daily practice. By making calm a habit, the more consistently you do it, like exercise, the better you'll feel and the easier it will be to keep going with it. The upside is that if you miss a day, it's not like all your hard work disappears. The benefits of your efforts and energy to maintain your health are still there even if you miss a workout.

The point is, be as proactive as you can be with planning but realize that you will sometimes need to bend and adapt. And the bending and adapting come with much less resistance, stress, pain, and suffering when you have a consistently charged battery and a solid practice of self-care and calm.

How we treat and fill our mind and body dictates our behaviors, habits, and connections with others. It also affects how we treat and show up for ourselves. When all areas are nurtured and cared for, we are able to own our calm and show up in the world as our best selves. **To reiterate, self-care isn't selfish. It is ensuring that your most important core circle is cared for, before you widen your circle.**

Here are some questions to consider:

- Is your body healthy?
- Is your mind healthy?
- Do you feel content?
- Do you have the resources you need to take care of your body and mind?

In general, are you doing well in those areas? If not, pause before taking on a responsibility that will distract you from taking care of yourself. I know this is easier said than done and as mothers we have people who rely on us. It is impossible to ignore others while focusing on your inner circle. But it can help you gauge where much of your energy should be and to give yourself even just five minutes of care before moving on to care for someone else.

For the first few years after we moved to San Francisco, my answer to "Are you happy where you are now?" was "No." I didn't feel content because I didn't feel a sense of belonging with my new community—I needed to better engage with where I lived. I remembered that I loved exploring and enjoying the area I live in and I'd stopped doing that after we moved. So I made it a point to take a hike or walk in a new place every week. I'd go into different shops and try different restaurants. When I did that, my connection with my new home deepened. I came to love the energy and environment, and I drew strength and peace from that. As I filled my self-care circle with these hikes (while also listening to audiobooks and music—that killing two birds with one stone thing again), I became stronger and more able to attend to the circles beyond me. It's so true that to make changes in the world, you have to start with yourself.

Sadly, not everyone has the most immediately supportive partners, which can make things much harder. If that's your situation, reference Getting Your Partner on Board on page 170. Maybe the dynamic between you and your partner was set years ago and this transition will be hard for them to accept because change can be uncomfortable. The work you did earlier in this book with roles and responsibilities and ambitions and dreams will help, because it's about both of you, not just yourself. But, if for some reason your partner is not on board, I beg you not to say, "Well, I guess I'll do that after the kids grow up and are out of the house," or "I'll do it if we break up." Instead, work on building a foundation that will make your ambitions and dreams happen, whether your partner is part of it or not.

Strategize time for yourself with the means you have. For example, it's common for a neighbor to watch your kids in exchange for you watching theirs. Get up early to enjoy the solitude of drinking a cup of tea and reading. Look for a higher-paying job so you can afford more third-party help if your partner is unable to step in. The cliché "Where there's a will there's a way" is true!

Taking Care of Your Body

There are two core areas of self-care: the body, and the mind and spirit. They all interconnect. When the body is well cared for, your thinking is clearer and your energy is higher. And when your mind is taken care of, it enables the body and spirit to be healthier as well.

Exercise

I love moving my body. I love the challenge of training, especially toward a goal like a triathlon. I love the meditative state my mind goes into when all it's focused on is one foot in front of the other on a trail. I love seeing my body level up when I work hard.

But let's be real: Having four kids puts a serious slowdown on even the most determined athletes. And I can imagine, if working out isn't your thing to begin with, how much harder it would be to make time to move your body.

Everyone knows exercising is good for the body. But did you know about the calming effect it has on the mind? It's been proven to cut stress and anxiety by reducing stress hormones (adrenaline and cortisol) and increasing the production of endorphins, that "ohhh, hell yeah" feeling you get after winning a game, getting good news, or relishing in some postcoital snuggling with your partner.

Too often, parents sacrifice their health for the well-being of their family. But how calm will the family be if your stamina is shot and you're snapping at everyone? How happy will the family be if you've had no outlet for your frustrations and are a wound-up tense ball of nerves?

I guarantee you—fitting in exercise will help in every single area of your life. It will help with sleep, creativity, and patience. It will help you feel accomplished, confident, and alive. It's something that no matter what other bonkers thing happens in your day, you can feel good about what you did.

I know you're thinking you have no time to work out, even if you are someone who wants to make that happen. And how in the hell do you fit it in, when you can't even have a full poop in the bathroom before someone is banging on the door because they "need" you for something? Well, my friend, it's time to whip out one of the main *Chaos to Calm* efficiency tools—your calendar—and look at the places in which you can fit in a few minutes here and there. As we also talked about in the Habits chapter (see page 62), when starting a new habit, keep it small! Don't forget to lean on your community to support you.

Here are more ways to make things happen:

Turn something that was sort of active into a workout. If you walk your kid to school in the morning, take the extra long route back home or turn your return walk into a jog. If you have a kid in a stroller, keep that stroller with your little one in it and take them along for the ride. You did all that work getting them out of the house, now make it count for you. And you don't need to show visual sweat on your shirt here; anything that moves your body is going to benefit you. Do you have to clean the house? Bust out your favorite Britney Spears and Dua Lipa playlist and turn it into a cardio burst. Do lunges at the dresser as you're putting away laundry. There are dozens of opportunities a week you can maximize to start moving more.

Do an activity that forces you to do it longer. Another avenue to incorporate more movement into your day is to do an activity that has no shortcuts or way for you to end early. Plan an exercise activity that doesn't have a shortcut to get out of it will help you stick with it. Find a favorite loop you can hike or run, and put in your calendar, such as "Canyon Loop" Once you're on the loop, it'll be harder, mentally, to turn around early, versus if you didn't make a plan and were just wandering around. Of course, if wandering the streets is something that fills your spirit with joy, by all means, do it! Some people find it easier to get a full workout if they join a class instead of being left to their own devices on the treadmill, walking at 1.5 miles per hour while watching *Love It or List It.*

Park at the back of the parking lot. You've probably heard this one, but it works! If you aren't in a rush, park in the back of the parking lot. Not only do you walk the extra minutes to the entrance, but then you have to walk yourself back to the car as well. Those steps add up!

YOUR TURN

Incorporating movement into your daily life?
Think about something you already have to do and how you can make it more physical. And don't forget to start small.

Here are some ideas to get your juices flowing:

- ☐ Walk or bike the kids to school instead of driving.
- ☐ Purposely leave something in your car so you are forced to go back for it.
- ☐ Take a dance break in between meetings.
- ☐ Get outside for a walk around the block between Zoom calls.
- ☐ Park at the farthest spot at the parking lot.
- ☐ Bike to the store instead of driving if you have a short commute (and a short list of things to get).
- ☐ Stretch in your bed before getting up for the day.

Recovery

Recovery is another form of self-care for the body. As much as it is important to move your body, it is also important to give your body rest. Recovery gives your body an opportunity to heal sore muscles pushed to their breaking point and fuse back together in a stronger way!

Active recovery. There is a concept in the endurance training world called "active recovery." The idea is that after strenuous exercise, unless you are injured, you don't stay sedentary while your body recovers; instead, you should move in a low-key, gentle way. This allows for the muscles to move while also letting them recover and grow stronger. When I was training for triathlons, I had built-in recovery days. Six days a week I had planned training days filled with running, biking, and swimming. One day each week was dedicated to recovery. But instead of using that day to binge-watch *Schitt's Creek*, my coaches told me to go for a walk or do yoga.

Sleep/rest. Another pretty obvious form of recovery is sleep. The importance of sleep is not news. Whether you've done research (like I have) or know it intuitively, you know that sleep is important and should be near the top of your priorities. We make sure our kids get sleep because we know what happens when they don't. Sleep is the ultimate recovery for both the mind and the body and it's vital in honing in on your calm. When your body is deprived of sound sleep, your bodily functions won't work properly and that will affect your ability to find, access, and be calm.

When I was in my twenties, I felt invincible. I could work out early in the morning, have a full productive day at work, and in the evening meet up with friends and stay out late, and repeat the next day. Oh boy, have things changed as I have gotten older. I no longer have the stamina of the Energizer Bunny and find myself needing to take longer breaks between activities. After painfully accepting that this is my reality, I now make sure that I don't plan back-to-back events. I generally keep to just one big event per weekend, or a minimum of one big event per day. Even just going shopping with my daughters is an event. And if you're recovering from an injury or have a new baby, just getting dressed can be an event.

If I know I have a physically demanding event to attend during the day, I plan to have a chill morning and evening. I might even plan to have a mellow next day to give my body the opportunity to rest. As you do your own planning, try not to schedule back-to-back nights out, or early mornings after one. Always plan for moments of quiet in between events.

One of the best ways to be successful in getting proper sleep and rest is to communicate that need to your family. As discussed in the Communication chapter (page 122), be proactive. Share with your partner that you're working on getting consistent sleep and that you would like to be in bed by a certain time. Share whether there's anything you need from them for this to happen. Maybe you need support with making lunches, getting the kids to bed, or loading the dishwasher. Tell your kids that you have a new bedtime, just like they do, and that you need their help to make that happen, in the form of them cleaning up their own rooms or putting on their pajamas.

Sleep/rest with a newborn/baby/toddler. Once you become a mom, the days of going to bed when you want are long gone. Remember when sleeping was interrupted only by the sound of the alarm or natural body rhythms, and you could wake up without a four-year-old staring down at you? Having children changes our relationship with sleep, especially when they are young. It is virtually impossible to get a solid night's sleep with a new baby, as they need to adapt to earth-side sleep patterns and feeding schedules.

Sleeping and resting are not easy when you are at the beck and call of a tiny being who can't talk, walk, feed itself, or use a toilet. So when it comes to sleep, don't fight reality; accept your new relationship with sleep. Calm can be found in your acceptance that sleeping through the night isn't going to happen for a while, and you'll need to be conscious about getting rest during the day. Take naps when you can and ask for help with chores and tasks so you can attempt to shut your eyes for even just a few minutes. I know it's frustrating to hear, "Sleep when the baby sleeps." Don't expect a deep nighttime sleep, but there is benefit to lying down with your eyes closed instead of using the time to tidy toys that will just get messy again. Fighting with reality by getting upset at your lack of sleep will only create suffering and chaos in your brain and body. Acceptance of reality actually creates calm.

When Sage was a few weeks old, a friend came over to hang out and catch up. While he was napping, she and I were chatting and I found myself dozing off. I told her that I could barely keep my eyes open and asked if she wouldn't mind hanging out and keeping eyes on Sage while I closed mine. To my delight she said yes! I got to nap, she got to quietly watch Netflix on her phone, and all was well with the world.

Nutrition and Food

Another self-care way to support your body in calm is to feed it well. Think about how good it feels to have a healthy meal and feel full of energy and ready to tackle whatever comes your way. Then think about the meals you had when you felt sluggish and lethargic afterward. Hello, food coma. When you are mindful about the foods you eat, it will contribute to the energy you want to have. With good nutrition and food habits, you will help create a natural state of consistent energy and will keep your battery running at optimal levels, which is an important factor in caring for yourself.

Foods that feed chaos and foods that feed calm. You know the drill, we are what we eat. If you want to be a greasy Big Mac, that's your prerogative, but I guarantee you won't feel energetic, sexy, and vital doing that. Turning chaos into calm requires you to set your body up for success.

When you have a sharp mind and eat to fuel your precious body, it will go a long way in getting to that calm space.

As we established in the Efficiency chapter (page 14), fresh whole foods are the best for fostering energy and promoting calm. When your body can easily digest and utilize the nutrients from food, it functions smoothly. Additionally, there are specific foods that are known to reduce anxiety and promote the release of serotonin and dopamine (the neurotransmitters for calm). When you include salmon, chamomile, turmeric, dark chocolate, yogurt, green tea, peanut butter, and oats in your diet along with whole, minimally processed foods that are high in antioxidants, your diet will support your brain health and overall well-being —self-care and nutrition double whammy!

Snacking isn't a particularly bad habit and, in fact, small meals eaten more frequently can be a great way to maintain energy levels. It's really the food that we consume that turns snacking from a friend into a foe. My top food tip for calm is to stop buying snacks and sweets that you know aren't good for you. If you don't keep them in your home or at work, you can't eat them. So don't buy them. I mean it. Stop it. It's not that you can't or shouldn't treat yourself occasionally, but you really don't need a daily Milky Way bar. If you stock your pantry or your desk at work with healthy goodies like nuts and fruit, that will be what you eat and once you get used to it you will be satisfied by them. Be sure to check out the list of foods that feed chaos and those that feed calm on page 23 or go to jennahermans.com/resources.

Pro Tip: Don't grocery shop on an empty stomach. You are more likely to make poor purchasing choices when you are hungry, grabbing foods that are convenient and "look" good. When you shop on a full stomach, you will be in a better place to make smart food choices. Additionally, if possible, do your shopping as early in the day as possible. When your brain isn't exhausted from making decisions all day, you'll shop more intentionally and be more likely to take your time and buy the foods you need instead of the treats you want. Treats always look more appetizing and appealing in the evening when your discipline is low. And I repeat: Don't allow yourself to have the treats in the house if your goal is to stop eating them. I know I can't trust myself around cookies at 8:00 p.m. But if that treat isn't in the house, I won't eat it because it isn't there!

YOUR TURN

As I mentioned in the Habits chapter (see page 62), the best way to remove a habit is to replace it with something else. As you think about your eating habits, what is one chaos-inducing food that you will replace with a calmer alternative? What is the alternative?

- ☐ Chaos Food _____
- ☐ Calm Replacement _____

Now go make it happen!

- ☐ Add to your calender when you are going to schedule self-care appointments as recurring.
- ☐ Add medical, dental, and therapy appointments into your calendar. And don't forget to set reminders.

Hydration

Being hydrated is incredibly important for helping the mind and body be calm. Dehydration can cause stress, and stress can cause dehydration (see Resources, page 252). The way to break this vicious cycle is by consistently drinking more water.

Here are two ways to know if you are dehydrated:

1. **Are you thirsty?** If you are, you're already dehydrated.

2. **Take a look at the bowl the next time you pee.** If your urine is dark in color, you're on your way to dehydration. The darker the urine, the more dehydrated you are.

The saying to drink eight glasses of water a day is outdated, but the sentiment is correct. In general, you should try to drink between ½ ounce and 1 ounce of water for every pound you weigh, every day. For example, if you weigh 150 pounds, that would be 75 to 150 ounces of water a day. If you're living in a hot climate and exercising a lot, you need to drink more, and if you're in a cooler climate and mostly sedentary, you need less.

BEST AND WORST DRINKS FOR ENERGY AND CALM.

The best are:

- Water
- Milk
- Fruit-infused water
- Coconut water
- Herbal tea

The worst are:

- Coffee
- Soda
- Energy drinks (e.g., Red Bull, Monster)
- Alcohol

Be careful with caffeinated drinks. Like everything else, moderation is key here, as caffeinated drinks tend to have a mild diuretic effect, causing the need to urinate. For the brain and body to be properly hydrated it is better to keep caffeine consumption to a minimum. Plus, shaky jitters from coffee definitely don't help your efforts for calm.

Here are some tips to help you drink more water:

- Carry a cute water bottle with you and fill it up throughout the day.

- Keep a glass or bottle of water on your desk at work.

- Keep a full glass or bottle of water next to your bed.

- Switch one can of soda or one cup of coffee for a glass of water or herbal tea.

- Drink small amounts of water often throughout the day.

- Keep a bottle of water in your car.

- If your bottle has a straw lid or pop mouth, keep the straw up and the mouth open. This will limit the number of barriers between you and the water.

If you hate drinking water. Try infusing water with fruit or veggies. It's hard for me to resist chilled cucumber water. You can slice up some oranges, lemons, strawberries, or mint (or a combination!) and make yourself a delightful beverage that also feels decadent and spa-like. Herbal teas are a great way to spice things up. Seltzer and sparkling waters (no, not the sugar-laden kinds, just plain or with essence added) are also non-boring ways of hydrating.

YOUR TURN

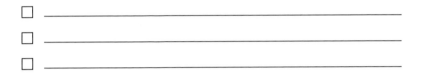

In your journal, write down how you will incorporate more hydrating liquids into your daily life.

☐ _____

☐ _____

☐ _____

Personal and Medical Care

The final self-care practice for your body is personal and medical care. Both of these tend to be things that busy parents push to the bottom of their to-do lists.

Personal care. There is no need to deny yourself things that make you feel good and at your best, like that haircut you've been wanting for months. And for regular self-care appointments like massages (if one is so lucky!), haircuts and color, facials, nails, doctor's appointments, and therapy, *book out six months at a time the next time you're at your provider.* When it's in the calendar, you will no longer stress about a last-minute realization that your gray hair has sprouted all over your head overnight the day before your anniversary dinner.

Medical and dental appointments. Just like you schedule your kids' medical and dental appointments on a regular basis, it is important that you get checked out regularly as well. As we get older, it's even more vital to have a doctor peek under the hood of your body vehicle and make sure everything is running smoothly. (Hello, proactive self!) Calm comes from knowing your engine is running well and there are no concerns about potential random heart attacks because you're making sure that your arteries are clear, your heart is pumping well, and your blood sugar is normal, along with everything else. If you have a chronic physical or mental health condition, it is especially important to schedule regular appointments to ensure that you are clinically checked and good to go.

The same goes for dental appointments. There's a reason why insurance companies cover two cleanings a year. If you have insurance, don't leave that money on the table—get those biannual teeth cleanings. And when you go regularly, you are more likely not to have major dental issues to deal with later on.

UMA
the unwell

My client Uma was struggling. She had no energy, was rundown all the time, and always seemed to have a cold that she just couldn't beat. She was irritable, anxious, and seemed to need more energy than most to do the basics like laundry and cooking. Although tired, she had a hard time sleeping, and over time this really took a toll on her mentally because she was too tired to go to her son's baseball games, go on date nights with her husband, and more. Additionally, she had inflamed lymph nodes in her neck that she explained were because her body was fighting off the cold of the moment. I asked her, if her kid was constantly sick and exhausted, what would she do about it? She said she would take him to see a doctor, to make sure that something else wasn't going on. I asked if her son had all of her symptoms, if she would wait to have him be seen or make an appointment as soon as she could, and she said she would take him the moment his lymph nodes were inflamed. "Do you not deserve to be seen by a doctor? What would your mother tell you to do if you told her about your symptoms?" I reminded her that just because she was busy and an adult with many responsibilities did not mean her health was not important or a priority. Taking care of herself was a key element of being able to live her best life, live in calm, and support the people most important to her.

She saw her doctor and was diagnosed with Grave's disease, a thyroid condition that causes (and explained her) sweating, difficulty sleeping, tiredness, and irritability. It also explained that the lump in her neck was not an inflamed lymph node, but a goiter—an enlarged thyroid gland. If left untreated it could lead to heart problems and weak and brittle bones. Of course it was hard to show up as her full self and give everything she had to herself and her family when her heart wasn't working properly, she was having sleep problems, and her bones were literally breaking. Uma sought treatment and ultimately was able to live a much better quality of life.

Nurturing Your Mind and Spirit

Okay, no eye-rolling, because I'm going to get a little woo-woo on you. You want to know how I can be calm and nurture myself while there is chaos around me every single day? This is it and I'm telling you what really works. So open up your mind and heart for a moment with me, my exhausted and maybe even slightly jaded friend.

Nurturing the mind and spirit are essential self-care practices and are two sides of the same calm coin. Just as important as taking care of your physical body is taking care of the intangible parts of yourself. You can have the healthiest body in the world—you exercise, eat well, get rest, and stay hydrated—but if your thinking is down in the dumps, you definitely won't be able to be your best self and own your calm. It is so incredibly important to nurture your mind and spirit, as they are what make you you and affect how you show up for everything. It's the difference between focusing on the thorns of a rose or on the aroma and beauty of the flower.

Self-care comes in to support your mind and spirit when you become aware of what feeds them both in a positive way. Taking care of your mind and spirit is an investment in your calm "bank account" with compounding interest; the more you put into it, the more you get out of it, and it builds on itself over time.

There are both internal and external ways to nurture these parts of you. Internal looks like the way you interact with your mind, while external are things you can do physically that are stimulating mental self-care.

Internal Nurturing of Mind and Spirit

How you approach your thinking affects the internal nurturing of your mind. Ways to practice internal nurturing include being kind to yourself, being quiet, allowing for active recovery, and practicing gratitude.

Be kind to yourself. This is an effective way to foster calm. What this looks like in action is saying affirmations, giving yourself permission to not be perfect, accepting yourself as you are, and not expecting yourself to act like, think like, or be like anyone else. Calm is achieved with radical self-acceptance, grace, and love. Tell yourself, "I am doing the best I can with what I have." When I get down on myself and feel like I am not doing enough or I'm falling short, I say those words to myself. I know I am perfectly imperfect and truly doing my best, and I know things won't always go the way I wish they would—I mean, I have four kids, work, and a partner, all expecting something different would be actual insanity.

Search out quiet space. Whether you call it meditation, rest time, or "Mommy's Mindfulness Minute," having a few moments to close your eyes and be still and silent is magic. Take deep breaths and connect with your body. This grounds you, and whether you do it before you get out of bed, before picking up kids from school, or before an important work meeting, this simple act will help you show up in your best way. I like to listen to guided meditations, and if I have a few extra minutes and feel like going longer, I will listen to gentle bells or other meditative sounds. When I am feeling stressed, I use the box breathing technique (breathe in for a count of four, hold for four, breathe out for four, and hold for four—then repeat). Even after just one round I feel better and it takes less than a minute to do. Try it and see for yourself how quickly it restores your calm.

I also highly recommend creating a small quiet space in or out of your home that you call your own. A friend of mine created what she calls her "sanctuary," which is a tiny patio space with a comfy couch where she goes to have even five minutes of quiet time.

Simply putting your phone on silent is an effective act of self-care when you need a break. It's actually a loving thing to do to not talk to someone when you're not feeling it, both for them and for you. Self-care can be not picking up the phone, not catching up with friends, or not expending more energy than is necessary. Taking care of yourself will sometimes look like clearing your calendar and doing the least amount possible or canceling plans in the name of self-preservation. Think about that "no" as a "yes" to the most important person in your life—you.

YOUR TURN

Creating space for quiet and calm

☐ Find a calming app that works for you.

- My favorite apps are Insight Timer, Healthy Minds Program, and Balance, though there are plenty of others available. You may have to try a few until you find the one that works for you.

☐ Find or create a quiet place in your home.

Pick a space in your home where you can go to sit quietly. Set out a chair or place a pillow on the floor, though you don't even need those if there is not enough space. If all you have is a wall, just make sure you have room to sit against it or lie next to it. Moments of silence don't require physical things, just for you to be comfortable. If you feel like it would be useful to have a timer or to use a meditation app, take a moment to do some exploring.

Active recovery of mind. Giving your mind time to recover after big events is just as important as giving your body rest after a big workout.

Especially when you do mental tasks and activities that you've never done before, you will get pushed to fatigue because you have not moved that brain muscle in that way or with that level of strength.

Our brains need energy, just like our biceps and quads. Maybe our brains don't get physically bigger when we exercise them in new and challenging ways, but the synapses and connections made in our brains grow and get stronger.

Your brain needs rest in between workouts so that you can show up to the next task with strength rather than weakness. Every mind is different, and when you schedule out your day, be mindful of your own recovery time. Figure out what cushion you can build in between tasks for active recovery. It could be ten minutes or two hours—you know what you need. Whatever your job is, whether you work in an office or at home as a full-time mom, your mind needs active recovery.

You may find you're getting demands from others when you know deep down you need active recovery time. Have the courage to tell them, "I'm unable to do that right now, but at xyz time I can address that." For example, my colleague's teen suffers from social anxiety and her mind truly needs to rest between functions, even those as simple as doctor appointments or going out to dinner. Since only she knows what her limits are, it's up to her to protect those limits. She'll tell her mom, "Can we reschedule piano lessons this week—it's the first week of school and I know I'll need extra recovery time."

Sometimes events happen that stress us out of the blue, and that's the time you can say, "I just need a quick walk around the block or a five-minute rest before I can go to the next thing." Do not ever feel guilt or shame or weakness for taking recovery time. That time you take for yourself will actually give you more strength to face whatever is next.

Active recovery in physical exercise is straightforward. You'd take a slow walk or do some light stretching. So what are some examples of how you do this for your mind?

- Play a calming song from your favorite playlist and close your eyes while you listen.

- Spend five minutes writing what you're grateful for today.

- Listen to a meditation.

- Use the time to breathe and reflect on the experience you just had, with a fresh and open mind.

For parents who are at home with kids, I totally know mental recovery is hard and you have to be more strategic about building in this time during naps or asking your partner or a friend to watch the baby while you decompress. Just knowing you have that to look forward to will make such a difference in your patience levels.

Recovery of your mind is key for mental self-care and is just as important as sleeping and eating. If you don't do it, just like if you don't rest the muscles in your body, you risk mental injury, like burnout, and not being able to do anything at all.

Gratitude journal. You've probably heard about gratitude journaling. Or maybe you've been knee-deep in dirty diapers and washing Dr. Brown's bottle parts and may have missed the trend. You know by now I'm all about efficiency and would never spend time on something that doesn't work, and I'm saying gratitude journaling is an effing game changer!!!

When you're connected to your gratitude, everything feels lighter, more positive, and easier to approach. It's an essence of being that reflects joy and positivity on all you perceive. Even with kids playing a game of "scream tag" while racing around you (hey, at least they're playing nicely and not trying to assault each other in the moment), or even if your partner has to work late (grateful for a steady income), and even when you are elbows-deep in your newborn's endless dirty diapers (baby's regular peeing and pooping are healthy signs!), you can find ways to see the good in the bad and you can change your perception of a disgusting, monotonous, normally annoying task. I don't say any of this to minimize your struggle. Whatever feelings you have are valid and relevant. What I am saying is that when you shift the perception of your reality to gratitude, it makes the hard things more bearable.

I write in a gratitude journal every night. And I don't just list the same sh*t over and over, like "I'm grateful for my husband and my kids and my job." That isn't where the essence or perspective change will come from. Perception change comes when you dissect the *reasons* behind your gratitude. Not just a vapid list of sh*t you know you should be grateful for but don't deeply (in the moment) feel. What you write doesn't have to be a novel, just getting one moment down on paper is all you need to feel the benefit.

Here's an example of what I wrote last night: "I'm grateful for my husband because he cooked dinner tonight. He saw how exhausting my day was and he cooked dinner for the family and cleaned the dishes afterward. It made me feel so grateful for our partnership."

This entry in my journal did a lot more for my body, mind, and soul than a simple listing of "I'm grateful for my husband" would be. After I wrote this, I thought about how good it felt to be seen, and how I could do that for him and the kids more.

Another example: "I'm grateful that my daughter told me about her day today. It was really stressful for her, and I feel badly that she's going through middle school drama. I'm so grateful she feels safe to share that with me, and that she and I have a close relationship where she trusts me."

No matter the drama, I can always be thankful my kids share with me, and it is a reminder that I don't always need to actively give advice or "parent" them. Sometimes it's enough just to show up, be present, and be an ear and a shoulder available for them.

You can find gratitude journals online and in the app store like Presently, Grateful, or Reflectly. You can use any note app, a Google doc, or a real-life blank notebook and pen.

YOUR TURN

—————————————   ✏   —————————————

Writing things down can help offload stressful feelings and organize your thoughts. Practicing gratitude will make you feel more grounded, ful-filled, and calm.

- ☐ Get yourself whatever journal works for you. Start the habit of writ-ing what you're grateful for, why, how it made you feel, and what it makes you appreciate, every day. Add journaling to your calendar and set a reminder so you won't forget.

External Nurturing of Mind and Spirit

Creative hobbies can redirect your stressed-out thoughts, or you can go outside your home and seek out friendships or volunteer opportunities. These are great options for when you have more time to devote to your self-care.

Hobbies. One way to nurture the mind and spirit is to practice hobbies or other activities that bring you joy. These are the things you do that feed your mind and spirit, like cooking, reading, drawing, or puzzles. Are you thinking, "Who has time for hobbies? I certainly don't." Oh, don't I know it.

Before kids, my hobbies used to include endurance training, cooking, reading, writing, and baking. All of a sudden I became a parent of three stepkids and then birthed our fourth, and pretty much all my hobbies either completely evaporated or felt like chores instead of enjoyable acts.

Instead of trying a new recipe for myself with some exotic new ingredient I got from the farmers' market, cooking turned into making whatever was quick and everyone would eat. I used to love drawing and painting but haven't played with my art supplies in who knows how long. My reading time evaporated faster than the frosting on a kid's cupcake. I felt emptier and pretty woe-is-me without having time to read in my life. Then I realized the joy of reading wasn't about finishing it (though, I'm not gonna lie, when I finish a book I feel very accomplished), but rather about the moments of quiet I enjoyed with just me, the smell of the binding, the pages fluttering through my fingers, and the thinking I did after reading a stimulating paragraph.

So I started reading for five minutes—just two pages at a time—at whatever times I could grab: nap times, rare moments when the kids were playing peacefully, while the kids were busy with Kyle, before bed. And I learned that just because you don't have a full hour to sit and read doesn't mean you can no longer be a reader or enjoy books. A book is read one page at a time and there is no rule that says you can't read even a paragraph at a time. Maybe at that pace you only read one book a year, but it's more than you would have done if you had accepted the idea that you didn't have enough time. What if in that one book, you learned something that could change your life? Plus, try listening to audiobooks, which you can do while you are running errands or exercising or chores. (Yes, yes, it's not the same as turning the pages, but it's important to work with what you have, not what you wish you had.)

> **Pro Tip:** My list of to-read books is so long I don't know whether I could cover it in a lifetime. One app I love to use that maximizes reading time (for nonfiction enthusiasts) is called Blinkist. Blinkist summarizes the key points of a book, so you can learn the main concepts in the book in fifteen minutes or less. If I enjoy the "blink" enough, like *The Subtle Art of Not Giving a F*ck* and *Bringing Up Bébé*, I'll go ahead and read the full version.

If you don't love to read, ignore everything I just said! *Chaos to Calm* is about making time to do the things you want to do, not what you don't want to do.

Hobbies are important for calm because they are a spirit-filling activity just for you. They are a respite from all of the endless to-dos and responsibilities. And you can watch them progress. If you love doing puzzles, doing just a few minutes a day will, over time, lead to a fully completed picture. What's great about hobbies is that there is no motive other than pure enjoyment. The goal isn't to get better, but to simply do something that brings you joy. You don't have to spend hours and hours on your hobby; you simply need some escape time for yourself, and that could be five minutes or five hours.

If you want to make your hobby a priority, you could join a group of fellow hobbyists. In addition to being around people with similar interests, you can build accountability partnerships with them. They can check in on you to see how you are coming along with your knitting, painting, musical instrument, or surfing.

YOUR TURN

- [ ] Write down a hobby you'd like to spend time doing regularly.
- [ ] Schedule time for it in the calendar.
- [ ] If possible, make it visible and easy to pick up and do whenever the opportunity presents itself.

Community time. As an introverted extrovert, I get a lot of pleasure and fulfillment from being with people and among my community. Being with people is a part of my self-care because I feel calm and grounded when I have a sense of belonging. There are days when I'll take my laptop to my favorite coffee shop or to the park and work there to feel the essence of my community around me. It brings me great joy to see a familiar face, wave at a neighbor walking by, or stop for a quick chat. I love that the barista knows my name and my usual order.

Friendships. I try to get together or have a catch-up call with one friend at least weekly so that I can connect with the parts of myself that aren't just mom, wife, and colleague. I know that one cup of coffee with a dear friend can fill me up for the rest of the day.

Religion/Spirituality. Other ways to connect with the community can be spending time with people at your place of worship. Here you are around people with whom you share at least one similar interest and can feel connected to something bigger than yourself.

Volunteering. Connecting with your community feeds your spirit (if you do as I suggested and choose your community wisely). When my spirit is in need of filling, I'll sign up to volunteer at the local food bank or go to the coffee shop and give $10 to the barista, $5 for them and $5 for the person behind me. Doing a kind deed is a win-win. You can also combine community and volunteering by volunteering at your kids's school or place of worship. Good feeling double whammy!

How to Start Caring for Yourself

Start Small

Self-care, like building habits, works best when you start small. And by small I mean so small that you can't help but succeed. However, there are times in life when even small advances feel like they are too much, and you "cave" into an old habit, which makes you feel guilty and weak. This isn't necessary! For example, perhaps you set a goal of self-care to limit sugar, and you start with intensions to skip cupcakes at all kids' birthday parties. And then, at Kendra's party, they served red velvet cupcakes from your favorite bakery. Your mouth drooled like an old bulldog looking at a sausage. You just had to have one and you enjoyed every morsel. Afterward, though, you felt the heaviness of guilt in your stomach like you had failed. But here's the thing—beating yourself up does not induce calm. At every juncture, ask yourself, "What feeds my calm here?" Maybe the cupcake *was* the calm-inducing factor for you that day! It doesn't mean you're going to start eating cupcakes at every meal.

Practice Kindness for Yourself

Self-care includes having compassion for yourself. When you sway from your goal, like eating that cupcake, you don't need to make yourself feel worse than you already do (which has more lasting detrimental physical effects than the cupcake itself, especially if you tend to spiral and unleash unhealthy behaviors when you are stressed, like drinking, overeating, or binge-watching shows).

Regret isn't always a bad emotion. It can be motivation to stay on track in the future. Stop beating yourself up over things you perceive as "wrong," and give yourself compassion and grace for being human. Practicing compassion for yourself will flex your calm muscle. Eating a cupcake (or whatever you think you failed at) is not a moment that should warrant so much upset that your cortisol levels rise. Save that for bigger issues! The stress of being upset about eating a cupcake will have longer-lasting effects than the calories you consumed. On a joyous and celebratory occasion, even if you're trying to cut back on sugar in general, let yourself enjoy the f*ck out of that cupcake.

Moving Through Big Emotions

There will be times when the days, weeks, and months just seem way too hard to do anything for yourself and when the emotions of life are overwhelming and too much to bear. It's okay to be angry; it's okay to be exhausted. It's okay to go to bed at 7:00 p.m. because you're just "done." It's okay to be sick of being stuck with lemons and having to make lemonade. Sometimes you want to make orange juice (or whatever you want to make) and not *have* to make lemonade. Or maybe, just once, you'd like to get handed a glass of juice you didn't actually have to make yourself. And throw some tequila in there while you're at it. Honestly, there are days where I'd give my left ovary for a strong margarita.

Feel your feelings. Acknowledge and accept them. Respect, process, and move forward. Easier said than done, of course, but that's part of the work of getting to calm. When you put self-care into practice, you'll have the ability and the tools to transform those lemons into something great.

What Happens in Your Body During Overwhelm

When in a stressful situation or when you have chronic stress, myriad things happen in your body all at once. Your heart rate increases, your breathing quickens, your muscles tighten, your brain releases adrenaline and cortisol, and your blood pressure rises. This is a physical survival response to protect your body from moments of danger, whether to prevent your own injury or to save your life or the life of another. This reaction to stress has served our species very well, like keeping early humans safe from hungry lions. Fortunately, modern humans don't typically have to worry about being eaten by a carnivorous cat, but we have other stressors in our world that activate the same stress response, like car accidents, arguments with partners, financial strain, traffic, and sick loved ones.

When I was in labor with Sage, I tried to deliver him without an epidural. Little did I know this was not going to go in my favor because I was given Pitocin, a synthetic hormone mainly used to stimulate contractions for mothers who are experiencing weak contractions or prolonged labor. I know you mamas who may have experienced this just put your hands on your uterus and cringed with me. For almost twenty-four hours after my water broke, I tried to manage the pain without intervention. But with the drug-induced unnaturally quick and strong contractions, I was lying on the floor screaming and I couldn't bear it anymore. I eventually got an epidural (thank the heavens), and as soon as I had relief from managing the pain, my whole body shook for two hours as the adrenaline left my system. That was the most extreme experience I ever had with how the body works under intense conditions.

A less extreme but more prevalent example of this was when I had to fire someone for the first time. For me, it was more stressful than breaking up with a boyfriend. My blood felt like it was filled with electricity. My skin felt hot, like it was burning up from the inside. I was so nervous about what the person's emotional reaction would be, especially because I had never let someone go before. I fully understood the ramifications of letting her go and that was a stress that ate at my insides. I was sweating like a sinner in church/a teenager hiding alcohol in their backpack/a turkey before Thanksgiving. Although I was 100 percent safe and not concerned that she was going to physically hurt me, it was hard to calm down my nervous system at that moment. In a fight-or-flight experience, cortisol is streaming through your body as if you're under attack, and your brain can't function properly because your body's resources are going to all your organs to preserve them and not necessarily to the brain (see Resources on page 252). So reacting and making decisions in this state is almost never going to be a thoughtful choice. And when the body is in this state for a prolonged period of time, it can lead to long-term physical harm.

When the body pulls from different resources without us being consciously aware, this limits our thinking capacity. When you have an argument with your partner, your kids aren't listening for the umpteenth time, or you have to tend to a playground wound, you may have noticed you had extra energy in the moment. But afterward, you were completely drained and wanted to sleep for days. That's because your adrenaline created energy that you did not typically use when you were in your normal state doing your normal stuff.

Self-care is a way to add energy back into your reserves so you can maintain homeostasis more often. When you practice self-care your reserves won't be as depleted when you come out of any stressful situations because you have been regularly refueling and being kind to yourself.

If you're going through an extra-stressful time, like having a baby or experiencing a loss, keep in mind that your mental and emotional health needs extra TLC and self-care. When I trained for triathlons, I had to eat more than usual and have additional rest and recovery time so I could show up well for the next training session. When you are running on empty, either physically or mentally, it's not possible to keep up, so you need to give yourself extra self-care.

You have to fill your mental energy reserves or you'll become that temper tantrum-y, ragey, hangry, say things you don't want to, yell at people, self-destructive person you've been trying *not* to be. You are an interconnected being with many elements that all need to work together to be whole. Being in a state of calm as often as possible allows you to do your best in all areas of life, including thinking. The brain works at its highest capacity when it's not under constant stress.

How to Regain Calm in an Overwhelmed Moment

The first thing to do to get yourself out of that fight-or-flight state is to flex your calm muscle. When you are in the moment, try to ask yourself, *Can I survive this? Is it temporary?* Most likely, the answer is, *Yes, it sucks, but it won't be forever and it won't kill you.*

Use a quick self-care method. If you have the time, practice a self-care ritual immediately, like repeating to yourself that you're safe while massaging your temples, practicing the box breathing technique (see page 242), singing a short song, stepping outside, or simply closing your eyes to calm down your nervous system.

Share big feelings. For bigger emotions, talking to a friend can help dissipate the stress. As I mentioned in the previous chapters, just the process of sharing and feeling heard can calm the mind and body. Don't look for a pity party or vent for the sake of attention—that definitely will not help. You don't need any negativity to be reinforced. What you need is a release of the internal pressure your body feels. Big feels are held in your body and they are like a water balloon. Your feelings balloon gets filled up and stretched so thin as the pressure builds that it feels like it's gonna pop. But by sharing your thoughts you can release some of the pressure and your feelings balloon can return to its more rested state. It's a little like having a good cry. You always feel better after letting out your tears, right?

Write it down. Journaling is also an incredibly effective modality for processing challenging moments and emotions. When I'm having a hard moment, I spew out all of the thoughts and emotions, either in a journal or in a notes app. No filter and no judging. The purpose of this is to get all my thoughts out of my head so I can create space to think about how to approach my situation and direct my thoughts in a much clearer and healthier direction. Write down all the things that you think you shouldn't or couldn't do or feel. This is only for your eyes, and you can even rip it up after you've worked through your issue if that supports your calm. Just because you feel a certain way in a moment doesn't mean you'll feel the same way after the moment has passed. The thoughts I write are just that—thoughts. They don't own me and they can change in an instant. They may not even be true—but it's cathartic to say and release them anyway. When you give your thoughts a chance to be acknowledged and to breathe, you can lay them to rest when you close the app or journal.

Many people think the goal of life is to attain 100 percent happiness. This isn't realistic. Trying to avoid negative thinking or to suffocate thoughts never helps, especially in the long run. The thoughts will just come back, bigger and angrier. Thoughts are like children. If you ignore them, they will keep trying to get your attention and they'll get louder and more disruptive until you finally acknowledge them. Once acknowledged and heard, they'll dissipate and move on. And also like children, thoughts don't need to be correct, they just want to be acknowledged. "Mom, did you know that the ocean is yellow!" Obviously it isn't, but Sammy just needed to tell you that so he could move on.

Get moving. Another great way to move through big emotions is to physically move your body. When I'm having big feelings, one of my favorite things to do is dance. I blast music (sorry not sorry, neighbors) and dance my heart out. I don't think about whether the dancing is good or bad, I just move. Sometimes I just end up jumping to the beat. Other times I make bigger hip movements, or my arms are going in all directions. It's quite the workout. The more I sweat, the better I feel afterward.

An even bigger expression of physically moving through big emotions is a concept called swamping, coined by Regena Thomashauer (aka "Mama Gena") in her controversially titled book *Pussy: A Reclamation*. Swamping is the process of physically moving emotions through the body, where you make your outside match your inside. If you feel like garbage, literally wear a garbage bag. Blast loud music and stomp around and pound pillows. This physical embodiment of how you feel internally will change your mental chemistry and jolt you with renewed energy (on top of looking and feeling ridiculous—you can't help but laugh at yourself).

With negative emotions, especially those based on prior hurts or stress, you can be triggered by the same situation repeatedly. If you don't appropriately feel and navigate through your negative emotions, they will keep resurfacing. But if you deal with your negative emotions in real time, work through them, understand them, and process them, the processing time for a repeat offense will be a lot quicker and less disruptive because your mind will remember the outcome from the last time you worked through it. Okay, that was esoteric! Here's an example.

IRIS
the irritated

Like many teenagers, Iris's sons were messy and didn't care about clothes and towels on the floor, heaps of dirty dishes, or trash bursting out of the bins. For more than a decade Iris cleaned up after her family with minimal help from her partner or children. As her boys got older, she's discussed the concept of sharing the household chores and responsibilities.

She shared her frustrations with them about their messy home and asked for their support in taking out the trash, hanging up their towels, putting their clothes in their hampers, and placing the dirty dishes in the sink. And even though she pleaded with them, they were not motivated enough to remember to follow through on their new shared responsibilities. Sound familiar?

One day Iris came home after a long day of work and found what felt like every dish in the house dirty and piled all around the kitchen. She even found heaps of dishes in their rooms, clothes strewn all over the floor, and wet towels on the floor of the bathroom. Yes, you guessed it, my friends: Our fellow mama Iris lost it. She screamed and told them she was disappointed in their behavior and their lack of respect for her and their home and she made a lot of threats of consequences.

Out of fear, the boys temporarily had a bout of motivation and cleaned the dishes and put their dirty clothes away. But old habits die hard, as we know. Iris and I talked about concepts like habit breaking, effective communication, and processing big emotions.

Iris said her biggest issue was the rage she felt every time her sons left a mess for her to clean up. Enter swamping and movement and gratitude journaling. I facilitated Iris through a swamp and afterward we talked through her anger. Her underlying feelings were focused on the disrespect and disregard she received from her family. It upset her when it appeared that no one cared about her feelings.

Through journaling and coaching she came to understand that:

1. She could be accountable for never having asked her kids to do chores prior to being teenagers. For the majority of their lives, they never had to participate in the household chores or take responsibility for their own belongings. After so many years without that expectation, they were being asked to suddenly do something different. No wonder it was hard for them to pick up this new habit of contributing to the care of their home.

2. She was able to be grateful that she modeled safety and household cleanliness for them. Clearly, her boys felt safe to be their messy selves and they had faith and trusted that there was someone who cared about them enough to clean up after them.

The next time she came home to a messy disaster, her rage was not as strong and dissipated much more quickly. She was able to recall the thinking she had done around building habits and expressing gratitude, and she was able to work through her frustration more quickly and with a lot more ease.

If you aren't in the space to do a deep dive into emotional overwhelm and you need some instant relief, here are a few quick calm hits to get you started:

1. **Put your hands on your heart.** Close your eyes. And just breathe.

2. **Open your hand, palm up, and use the index finger on your other hand to make gentle circles in your palm.** Feels good, doesn't it?

3. **Do box breathing.** As I described earlier, this is breathing in for a count of four, holding your breath for a count of four, breathing out for a count of four, and holding your breath again for a count of four. Repeat this as often as you can within the time you have. I recommend doing this at least three times in a row. It takes less than one minute to complete three cycles of four-count box breathing.

Reduce Cortisol So You Can Respond, Rather Than React

When you use one of the methods above, it will reduce the amount of cortisol and adrenaline in your body so you can approach whatever is happening with the ability to give yourself space to think clearly and respond thoughtfully rather than have a knee-jerk response. This will slow down your heart rate and give your body the chance to assess the situation and take a beat before responding.

AUDREY
the angry

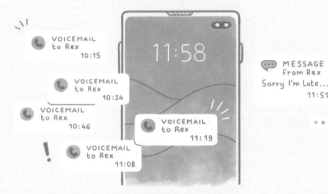

My client Audrey reached out to me because she had feelings of constant anger and she lost her temper more often than she wanted. Her three kids were incredibly challenging, and she ran on empty pretty much all the time. Audrey is a single mom, and she worked hard to support her family. Her ex-partner, while amicable and well intentioned, was inconsistent with child support and unreliable when it came to being with the kids due to the nature of his job.

Audrey hated that she would get excessively angry every time her ex missed a payment or was late to pick up the kids. It affected her mood for the rest of the day, and she hated how it monopolized her happiness and chased away her calm.

I had Audrey practice writing down her feelings immediately when they occurred, no matter what thoughts or emotions came up. Once she started she actually dictated into her phone because she couldn't type her feelings fast enough. We joked that the dictation should be in all bold and caps because often she was yelling into the phone. But we figured that it was better for her to unload to herself in an app than to an undeserving stranger who accidentally stepped on her foot or took the last croissant at the coffee shop.

After Audrey's first week of journaling, we talked about it. Her writings usually started with something like, "I can't believe he didn't pay on time again! He needs to get a better job with consistent money. He needs to pay for the kids too. I am not made of money," and would end with "Thank goodness my job pays enough where I can take care of the children and afford to cover our expenses until he is able to pay. Thank goodness I have a family who is willing to help out if I need it. I see that Rex (the ex) is working hard and paying me as soon as he gets paid. He isn't trying to get out of his child support responsibilities."

She shared that writing through her thoughts was cathartic, it made her anger dissipate more quickly, and she was better able to let it go and move on with her day; she even felt gratitude afterward.

Sometimes, when painful issues are recurring and there is deeper emotional rupture and pain, and writing down your feelings is not enough, a stronger intervention is needed. Maybe you need to talk to someone, whether it's a friend or family member or a professional, like a therapist or coach. You can refer to your writing to help you articulate how a challenge makes you feel. After you've written down your emotions as you were feeling them and with your whole heart, sharing pieces of it can be useful for your trusted person to understand where you're coming from so they can provide the best support.

If your big emotions are stemming from someone else's actions, you can use your writing to help you share those feelings with the person who elicited them. As was the case for Audrey, she used to get so mad at her ex when he was late with the child support money. After her first week of writing down her extreme feelings, she shared her emotional process with Rex by telling him, "I am sorry for getting so mad at you. I know you are doing your best. This is a really challenging time for all of us. As I processed my reaction and my feelings about how you were late with the child support, I realized that even though you were late, you still bring it and I see that you are working hard to make that happen. Thank you."

YOUR TURN

☐ What method are you going to practice when you need immediate calm?

☐ In your journal, write down your plan for how to move through your big emotions the next time they cause chaos in your mind and spirit.

OWN YOUR CALM: SELF-CARE RECAP

Self-care is a key element for owning your calm because it fills your energy reserves and makes you a priority, which enables you to show up as your fullest, most capable self in all areas of your life. By caring for yourself physically, mentally, and spiritually, you will be able to more easily respond rather than react, recognize your energy flows, and avoid or take care of issues when they are small, before they grow.

Ensuring you are cared for means you won't get overly depleted. You'll be able to let go of resenting that no one else is making you a priority. You can take care of your basic human needs, and from a place of fulfillment and calm (through movement, nutrition, hydration, rest, recovery, and emotional well-being practices), you'll notice a stronger, calmer, more resilient you.

Moving forward with Calm

FRIENDS, DOING THE BEST YOU can is truly the best you can do. As long as your heart is facing forward with love (not only toward others but toward yourself as well) and with integrity, you are doing what you need to do.

Wherever you are in the *Chaos to Calm* mission is right where you're supposed to be. In this book, we covered a lot of ground, but my goal for you is not to be overwhelmed. You're going to start small and tackle one thing at a time. The concept of doing it all and having it all is bullsh*t. It is a lie that anyone can do everything and keep all the balls in the air without ever slipping. It's a facade.

As humans, we feel everything. We may not show our true feelings in every moment, as we have to be present for whatever is needing our attention at the time. Sometimes we squash those tears of sadness about a lost friend while we're cheering our kid on during their baseball game. We cry with our child when they're relaying a story of being teased and squash the excitement about the promotion we got that day. But we *feel it all*, and we're supposed to.

What you *can* do is set your life up to make more space for mindfulness, kindness, and calm to yourself by being efficient, being proactive, creating small healthy habits, communicating effectively, harnessing your community, and taking care of yourself.

Give yourself permission to be a work in progress. I'm not perfect. And I have no desire to strive for it. **Perfection is fleeting and unsustainable and unrealistic.** But progress! Progress is something we can accomplish. We can show up for those who need us, and most importantly, we show up for ourselves. It's okay to be satisfied that things are never perfect. What does exist is progress and practice, and by using the methods in this book, you can find them.

The situations that require extreme energy and attention in one moment may not need them the next. On some days, work may take up more time than family; sometimes family will need more attention than work. Your relationship with your partner may need more attention on one day than the next. Or one kid may need more attention than another, and then it flips. The yin and yang are always moving. Energy is always flowing. You've got this! You have people rooting for you, and at the very minimum, you have me and the pages of this book.

No one is an island. Look for those who show up for you in your *Chaos to Calm* journey. Add them to your core community list. The only reason humankind has progressed as much as we have is because we've done it together, with teamwork, support, and compassion.

By you doing this courageous work, you are setting the stage for others to do the same. You are granting permission for other overwhelmed parents and you are modeling for your children that it's okay to put themselves first. To know that *their own* calm is important and they need to take care of themselves. Fostering calm is not selfish.

Calm is there for everyone, just like courage is. There is a lot of crap in between you and calm sometimes, but calm is always there. Calm is a muscle, and the more you exercise it, the easier it will be to find.

You are filled with every single thing you need to live the life you want to live, not just the life your kids or partner or boss or parents want for you. I am rooting for and am here for you. You are welcome to email me, direct message me, or connect with me on any social media outlet. I see you. You are loved. You are supported. And we are all in this together.

My friend, my beautiful, lovely, spark of a friend. It's time to shine—in calm.

YOUR TURN

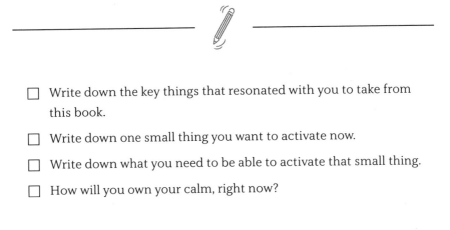

- ☐ Write down the key things that resonated with you to take from this book.
- ☐ Write down one small thing you want to activate now.
- ☐ Write down what you need to be able to activate that small thing.
- ☐ How will you own your calm, right now?

Resources

SLEEP AND DEPRESSION

Babson, K. A., C. D. Trainor, M. T. Feldner, and H. Blumenthal. "A Test of the Effects of Acute Sleep Deprivation on General and Specific Self-Reported Anxiety and Depressive Symptoms: An Experimental Extension." *Journal of Behavior Therapy and Experimental Psychiatry* 41, no. 3 (2010): 297–303. https://www.ncbi.nlm.nih.gov/pmc/articles/PMC2862829.

"Depression and Sleep: Understanding the Connection." Johns Hopkins Medicine. https://www.hopkins-medicine.org/health/wellness-and-prevention/depression-and-sleep-understanding-the-connection.

"There's a Strong Link Between Anxiety and Depression, and Sleep Problems, and It Goes Both Ways." *The Conversation*, May 11, 2017. https://theconversation.com/theres-a-strong-link-between-anxiety-and-depres-sion-and-sleep-problems-and-it-goes-both-ways-76145.

POSTPARTUM DEPRESSION

Carberg, J. "Postpartum Depression Statistics." PostpartumDepression.org, March 21, 2022. https://www.postpartumdepression.org/resources/statistics.

PARENT-CHILD COMMUNICATION

Eyberg, S. M., M. M. Nelson, N. C. Ginn, N. Bhuiyan, and S. R. Boggs. *Dyadic Parent–Child Interaction Coding System*, 4th edition. Gainesville, FL: PCIT International, 2013.

EXERCISE AND MOOD

"Exercising to Relax." Harvard Health Publishing, July 7, 2020. https://www.health.harvard.edu/staying-healthy/exercising-to-relax.

DEHYDRATION AND STRESS

Shaw, G. "Water and Stress Reduction: Sipping Stress Away." WebMD, July 7, 2009. https://www.webmd.com/diet/features/water-stress-reduction

FIGHT-OR-FLIGHT RESPONSE

"Understanding the Stress Response." Harvard Health Publishing, July 6, 2020. https://www.health.harvard.edu/staying-healthy/understanding-the-stress-response.

"What Happens to Your Body During the Fight or Flight Response?" Cleveland Clinic, December 9, 2019. https://health.clevelandclinic.org/what-happens-to-your-body-during-the-fight-or-flight-response.

ADDITIONAL RESOURCES

Go to jennahermans.com/resources/ or use the QR code to go to Jenna's website and find:

- Roles and Responsibilities Chart
- Overnight Oats Recipe
- Weekly Meal Planning Chart
- Habit Tracker
- Foods That Are Energy Friends + Foods That Are Energy Enemies

Acknowledgments

Thanks go to:

MY MOTHER—You show me every day how to choose peace, love, and generosity above all else. You are the best person I know and are my role model for calm. **MY CHILDREN**—I wouldn't have my path to calm without you. Without your presence, love, support, and understanding, I wouldn't have asked the questions, experienced the challenges, and searched to find solutions. Thank you for being my guinea pigs and my favorite people. **KYLE**—Your unwavering love and support gave me the wings I needed to be courageous in every aspect of my life and to follow my dream of making this book. My partner in all the things, you show and prove to me every day that anything is possible. **SHANNON**—I would have been lost in seas of words without you. Your superpowers, humor, and companionship made creating this book a joy. **STEPHANIE AND ELIZABETH**—Thank you for sharing all the highs and lows and everything in-between. **THE COLLECTIVE BOOK STUDIO**—Amy, for beautifully guiding my every step along the way; Angela and the whole CBS team, for taking me on as an author, seeing the worth of this book, and supporting the manifestation of my life's purpose in book form. **MY CLIENTS**—Thank you for being courageous to own your calm and for sharing your stories and lives with me.

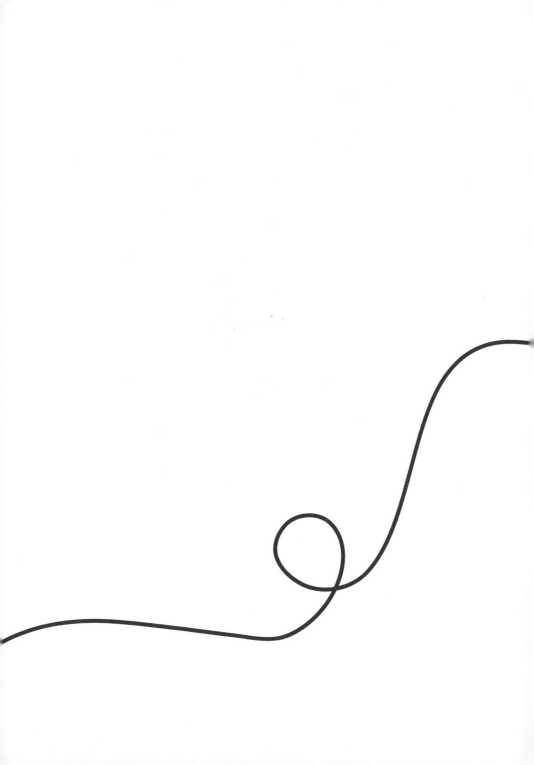

About the Author

Jenna Hermans is living proof that you can create a life of calm within chaos and overwhelm. She uses her bachelor's degree in Psychology, master's degree in Organizational Management, and 15+ years of human resources experience to build strong teams and company cultures, which she uniquely applies to her home life as well as work. Jenna is co-founder and COO of Be Courageous and founder of Chaos to Calm Coaching. She manages the businesses, family operations, and kids' schedules, all while nurturing her sanity and well-being, and promoting calm. She lives in the San Francisco Bay Area with her husband and four kids.